The City, the River, the Bridge

The City, the River, the Bridge:
Before and after the Minneapolis
Bridge Collapse
was sponsored by

**Office of the Senior Vice
President for Academic Affairs
and Provost**

**University of Minnesota
Institute for Advanced Study**

INSTITUTE FOR
ADVANCED STUDY

UNIVERSITY OF MINNESOTA
Driven to Discover℠

**University of Minnesota
Institute on the Environment**

INSTITUTE ON THE
ENVIRONMENT

UNIVERSITY OF MINNESOTA
Driven to Discover℠

University of Minnesota Press

The City, the River, the Bridge

Before and after the
Minneapolis Bridge Collapse

Patrick Nunnally, Editor

Preface by E. Thomas Sullivan

University of Minnesota Press
Minneapolis • London

Published by the University of Minnesota Press
111 Third Avenue South, Suite 290
Minneapolis, MN 55401-2520

http://www.upress.umn.edu

Library of Congress Cataloging-in-Publication Data

The city, the river, the bridge : before and after the Minneapolis bridge collapse /
Patrick Nunnally, editor ; preface by E. Thomas Sullivan.
    p.   cm.
  Includes bibliographical references and index.
  ISBN 978-0-8166-6766-6 (hc : alk. paper)
  ISBN 978-0-8166-6767-3 (pb : alk. paper)
1. Minneapolis (Minn.)—Social conditions. 2. Minneapolis bridge collapse, Minneapolis, Minn., 2007. 3. Bridges—Mississippi River—History. 4. Mississippi River—History.
I. Nunnally, Patrick.
  HN80.M6C57 2010
  363.12'5—DC22

                2010047369

Design and production by Mighty Media, Inc.
Text design by Chris Long

Printed in the United States of America on acid-free paper

The University of Minnesota is an equal-opportunity educator and employer.

17 16 15 14 13 12 11   10 9 8 7 6 5 4 3 2 1

Contents

This Dynamic Culture of Learning

E. Thomas Sullivan

On August 1, 2007, just after 6:00 P.M., during the evening rush hour in Minneapolis, the 1,900-foot-long, eight-lane I-35W bridge buckled and crashed into the Mississippi River. Massive plumes of dense smoke and dust filled the air. A mighty interstate bridge of concrete and steel had fallen suddenly, and the shock and pain were felt in the Twin Cities, across the state, and around the world. Thirteen people died, 145 were injured. The unimaginable had happened—right here on the doorstep of our University of Minnesota Twin Cities campus.

The worst brought out the best. In typical Minnesotan spirit, many in our university community responded immediately. Rushing to the scene were those from our medical, nursing, and dentistry communities. In addition to campus police and emergency personnel, faculty, students, and staff arrived quickly on the scene to assist. Support was provided by students and staff from our Duluth and Morris campuses. In ways both large and small, our university community participated heroically, persevering in the midst of a powerful scene of chaos and disbelief. Later, research and engineering teams arrived to review the wreckage, search for causes, and begin planning for the future. When we think about what these and so many others who teach, study, and work at the university contributed, I know we can all be proud of them and who we are as a university community.

At the university, we began to coordinate a longer-term institutional and academic response, recognizing that an understanding of complex and critical twenty-first-century issues requires that we cross academic and institutional boundaries. We have become much more nimble, bringing together interdisciplinary teams of scholars, practitioners, and performers to work side by side with each other and with local governmental, private, and nonprofit partners to form new problem-solving alliances across areas of expertise. These efforts model the kind of civic engagement and collaborative and integrative discovery processes that are so central to our mission as a public research university.

In its broadest sense, this book was developed to answer a critical question: what can we, as a great public research university in an equally great community, do to identify and communicate the longer-term impacts and implications of the I-35 bridge collapse?

As Nobel Laureate Professor Toni Morrison wrote, "We teach values by having them."[1] At the University of Minnesota one of our core values is to work as faculty, students, and staff in partnership with our external communities to solve pressing local and regional problems of national and international significance. The I-35 bridge collapse makes for a perfect case study. This book is a remarkable opportunity to convey and underscore our university's commitment to real-world solution-based research, teaching, and engagement. In short, this book exemplifies how we, as an institution, teach values by having and modeling those values.

Although universities are often mischaracterized as places deeply resistant to change, great universities have proven to be enduring institutions precisely because they have responded to long-range issues affecting the public good in creative, deliberate, and consultative ways. We understand at the University of Minnesota how to learn collectively and independently within an environment of change and when facing the unexpected. Universities understand

and exemplify this dynamic culture of learning in ways that many other entities cannot.

It may be that our newest members of the University of Minnesota arrive on our campus by way of the new I-35 bridge with little or no memory of what happened on that first day of August in 2007. But this book can act as a potent, meaningful, and tangible reminder of the magnitude and levels of meaning of that complex event and its implications across time and space.

We have a role, I might say a duty, as a major public research university to consider and take into account both a broad temporal and spatial academic range. What does it mean to "think like a university" when faced with a problem of such impact and magnitude? What have we learned? What is there still to learn?

Published by our University of Minnesota Press, this book attempts to answer these and many more questions from a variety of perspectives and methodologies. It also demonstrates the leadership role of the university not only in discovering new knowledge but in preserving and disseminating it. After reading this book, I trust you will appreciate the enduring and immeasurable value of what great public research universities contribute to the world and to the public good, working in concert with local, national, and global communities.

NOTE

1. Toni Morrison, "How Can Values Be Taught in the University?" in *What Moves at the Margin: Selected Nonfiction*, ed. Carolyn C. Denard (Jackson: University of Mississippi Press, 2008), 195.

University Voices in the Community

Patrick Nunnally

It is easy to overlook one salient fact about institutions such as the University of Minnesota: they are *placed*, that is, they contribute to the life of the community in which they exist. In the modern world of digital, global communications, where scholars can engage in simultaneous discourses with colleagues across the country and around the world, the fact remains that the university itself, the physical buildings and components of the campus and the people engaged in the day-to-day activities of teaching, learning, and research, exists as part of a larger community. Whether that larger community is a robust metropolitan region, a small town surrounded by fields or forests, or something in between, the community is part of the life of the university and vice versa. Despite the inroads of virtual, online colleges and courses of learning, American higher education, at this time anyway, remains at least implicitly a matter of community-university interactions.

This fact matters, and for more than the apparent reasons of the university providing sports teams to entertain the community and a payroll that supports local jobs. For better or worse, universities are

critically important institutions in the life of their communities. I
use the phrase "critically important" deliberately, for one of the civic
functions of a university is to serve as a critical voice, asking difficult
questions that often get overlooked in the scrum of everyday community development, political, and economic activity. It is sometimes up
to the university, through various means, to ask: Can we do this better? Have we thought this through carefully enough?

There is another, more immediate sense in which universities are important to their communities, and that is when disasters
strike. After Katrina hit New Orleans in the fall of 2005, Tulane closed
for a semester but reopened in January 2006. Since then, the university has been one of the pillars of New Orleans' rebuilding efforts,
contributing leadership and human effort in fields as diverse as medicine, education, engineering, and planning. Tulane president Scott
Cowen was quoted in a *Time* magazine report on university presidents: "One of the critical decisions we made was to integrate public service into the university's core curriculum so that every student
would engage in public service for all four years."[1] Higher education's
response to Katrina was by no means limited to the local universities; schools from across the nation have sent student teams, conducted collaborative research, and otherwise been heavily engaged
in focusing their intellectual capital on issues raised by the storm
and the recovery and rebuilding efforts. The Penn Institute for Urban
Research convened two conferences in the year after Katrina focusing on the complex conceptual, political, economic, and related issues
posed by urban disasters. Two books came out of that work, one of
which, *Rebuilding Urban Places after Disaster*, assembled nearly two
dozen essays confronting a range of policy and conceptual problems
posed by the efforts to rebuild New Orleans and the parts of the Gulf
Coast destroyed by the storm.[2]

In a small way, the present volume follows a similar pattern. In
this book, eleven scholars associated with the University of Minnesota all offer professional and personal reflections on the aftermath
of the I-35w bridge collapse. The book's chapters are modifications of
a series of presentations at an October 2008 symposium at the Uni-

versity of Minnesota, where scholars and public officials reflected on what we as a community might have learned as a result of the collapse and the series of events following it that led to the speedy replacement of the downed bridge. Participants were encouraged to take a long view: In ten or twenty years what will we likely be thinking about as we look back on this time? Are there particular lessons learned? Roads not taken or opportunities missed? Did the bridge collapse and rebuilding effort cause us to think in new ways about the bridge and our transportation system? About the city? About the Mississippi River?

The answers, of course, as these essays demonstrate, are both yes and no. Thomas Fisher, the dean of the University's College of Design, in chapter 1, "Fracture-Critical: The I-35w Bridge Collapse as Metaphor and Omen," sees the downed bridge as a metaphor for what he terms our "fracture-critical" society. Fisher's essay, which led off the October 2008 symposium during a week that the stock market was in freefall, is a trenchant reminder of the underlying conceptual structures that guide our behaviors and institutions. When we build anything—be it a bridge or a financial system—without redundancy and safeguards, we are asking for disaster.

But why, exactly, did the bridge fall? It certainly wasn't designed to be unstable, but was the disaster the result of a design error, weak materials, overloading, or some combination of factors? Roberto Ballarini and Minmao Liao of the Civil Engineering Department in chapter 2, "The Infamous Gusset Plates," detail specifically the results of an investigation, conducted with student assistance, of what the likely cause of the bridge collapse was. This study, which reached the same conclusion as investigations conducted by the National Transportation Safety Board and by consultants hired by the Minnesota Department of Transportation (MN/DOT), offers another critically important function of the university: to teach the brightest young people so that they can be important contributors to society.

The process of building a new bridge after such a public and widely publicized disaster is fraught with tension even in the best of times. As I note in chapter 3, "Building the New Bridge: Process and Politics in City-Building," the period between August 2007 and September 2008, during which the new bridge went up, was a time rife with political sniping, very public questioning of the decision making and assumptions that MN/DOT exercised in creating the new bridge, and wondering about what had gone wrong. Through all of this, MN/DOT and its consultants persevered, creating a bridge that surpassed the older one in many ways, even though it did not live up to the perhaps unrealistic hopes that many people had for it.

Urban bridges pass through neighborhoods and connect parts of the region. The book's next two essays take up expanding scopes of inquiry. Judith A. Martin, an urbanist and resident of the neighborhood in the immediate vicinity of the bridge, writes in chapter 4, "Neighborhoods Confront a Disaster Aftermath," how many of the everyday living patterns of urban life were disrupted by the gigantic construction project that suddenly appeared. She laments the missed opportunity for suburban commuters to learn more about the community they drove through on their rerouted path, which took them onto city streets rather than passing through on the freeway. Missed opportunity is likewise the subject of geographer Roger Miller's chapter 5, "From Here to There to Nowhere: Competing Philosophies of Planning." Miller argues that a series of "roads not taken" in twentieth-century urban planning has left us in a position where the rupture of one link in a complex regional transportation system becomes a disaster of wide consequences.

John O. Anfinson, a University of Minnesota graduate who now serves as a historian with the National Park Service (the Mississippi River in the Twin Cities is a unit of the National Park Service, the Mississippi National River and Recreation Area), in chapter 6, "A Fickle Partner: Minneapolis and the Mississippi River," provides a historical perspective on disasters associated with the Mississippi River in this area. Anfinson points out that despite past disasters that resulted in hundreds of deaths, public policy has changed very slowly, and he wonders how much we really notice and take account of the Mississippi River.

A theme that might be termed the "overlooked" Mississippi runs through the next two chapters. Mark Pedelty, a professor in the School of Journalism and Mass Communication, and Heather Dorsey and Melissa Thompson, in chapter 7, "A Bridge to Somewhere," note that, unlike the saturation of media coverage that accompanied the bridge collapse, a longer-term disaster of perhaps greater consequence takes place every summer in the Gulf of Mexico. They refer to the hypoxic zone, or dead zone, a substantial area in the Gulf that is so saturated with contaminants flowing from the Mississippi River that marine life cannot survive. Of course, the 2010 oil disaster brought unprecedented media and policy attention to the pollution problems of the Gulf, but the larger point raised by Pedelty and his colleagues remains: many of the most basic, unquestioned assumptions about our ways of life end up poisoning our waters, and we hardly are aware of these connections.

Deborah L. Swackhamer's chapter 8, "Old Man River," reiterates arguments about our damage to the river that sustains us. Swackhamer is an internationally reknowned water chemist and professor of science, technology, and public policy who suggests that, because of the collapse, we now know at least that the Mississippi River flows through our community.

By way of conclusion, I offer the suggestion that we have not yet really learned to see and understand the river that flows through the city of Minneapolis. It is true that there has been economic development oriented toward the river for several decades, but we don't yet fully design our cities as if the river is centrally important. Some programs are making steps in that direction, though, and those programs and the people driving them give us great hope for a sustainable urban Mississippi River.

The symposium that was the basis of this book in turn grew out of a course and public lecture series held in the fall of 2007, within weeks of the collapse and as the mechanisms to rebuild the bridge were being set in motion. I was asked to teach the class and formulate the lecture series in part because I was the junior staff member in the room when it was decided to have a class and series, and in part because my scholarship and public work over the past fifteen years has been on the Mississippi River. The class, cosponsored by the Provost's Office, the Urban Studies Program, and the College of Design, offered students the opportunity to reflect on community responses to the bridge collapse in real time, as policies and politics were informing decision making, rather than after the fact as a historical case study. The twenty-four students who signed up for the course and developed "river stories" out of their studies truly got a firsthand look at how cities respond to emergencies and how decisions made in the heat of a crisis will have long-term implications for many elements of our daily life that are all too often unreflected on. My essay on the building of the new bridge owes a great deal to the students and teaching assistants associated with the course and to the lecturers who were good enough to offer their thoughts on the importance of the city, the river, and the bridge in the Twin Cities.

NOTES

1. *Time* magazine, "10 Best College Presidents," http://www.time.com/time/specials/packages/article/0,28804,1937938_1937933_1937918,00.html#ixzz0XbSXE4TW (accessed November 22, 2009).

2. Eugenie L. Birch and Susan M. Wachter, eds., *Rebuilding Urban Places after Disaster: Lessons from Hurricane Katrina* (Philadelphia: University of Pennsylvania Press, 2006).

PART I

The Bridge: Object, Metaphor, Process

CHAPTER ONE

Fracture-Critical: The I-35w Bridge Collapse as Metaphor and Omen

Thomas Fisher

At rush hour on August 1, 2007, the 1,907-foot-long I-35w bridge near downtown Minneapolis suddenly fell into the Mississippi River, killing 13 people, injuring 145 more, severing a key link in the interstate transportation system, and costing over $300 million in damages and in the building of a new bridge.[1] After over a year of investigating the possible causes of the collapse, the National Transportation Safety Board concluded in its report that the engineers who designed the bridge in the early 1960s had undersized the gusset plates that connected the segments of the bridge's steel. That error, compounded by the weight added to the bridge over time with extra lanes, and repaving equipment and materials on the day of the collapse, led to the failure of the span. In a matter of a few seconds, 456 feet of the bridge fell 108 feet into the river, taking with it 111 vehicles.[2]

Experts estimate that some 465 bridges in the United States have designs similar to that of the I-35w span, and the inspection and reinforcement of those structures has become vitally important as this country embarks on a nationwide upgrading of its infrastructure.[3] However, we need to see the I-35w bridge and all of the other spans

FIGURE 1.1 » The collapsed I-35W bridge after initial recovery efforts had been completed and site preparation had begun, August 15, 2007. Author's photograph.

like it not as an isolated issue, having to do just with bridge design in the post–World War II period, but instead as part of a much wider problem that characterizes much of the infrastructure and development that we have put in place over the last sixty years: a problem of fracture-critical design.

When engineers define a structure as fracture-critical, they refer to its susceptibility to complete collapse should any part of it fail. A fracture-critical design has four key characteristics, the first of which is a lack of redundancy. The undersized gusset plates on the I-35W bridge might not have brought the entire span down if it had had enough additional structural members to carry the entire load of the bridge even if some part of a truss failed. At the time of the bridge's design in the early 1960s, such a redundant structure might have seemed unnecessarily expensive and wasteful. However, given the extraordinary expense of replacing the entire bridge after its complete collapse, the relatively small incremental increase in cost of adding redundant structural elements at the time of its initial construction would have been a much more cost-effective investment. Bridge designers now understand that, and over the last few decades, they have increased the redundancy of bridges, but the pressure to keep initial costs low remains a constant threat to the resiliency of our infrastructure.

The vulnerability of fracture-critical designs to complete failure also comes from their interconnectedness and efficiency. The I-35W bridge had both. The cracking of the gusset plates near the southern end of the bridge led to the overstressing and subsequent failure of other gusset plates and truss members, all of which were interconnected as part of a single structure in such an efficient design that nothing could interrupt the serial collapse. The Tenth Avenue bridge adjacent to the I-35W bridge shows what a less interconnected and less efficient design entails. Completed in 1929, that bridge has several independent concrete arches, separated by large concrete pylons that divide the structure into discrete parts. At the same time, the myriad concrete columns supporting the road deck all seem oversized for the load they carry, making the entire ensemble less than efficient but more than sufficient to compensate for the failure of any one element.[4] Even if a number of columns or one of the arches were to fail, the entire bridge would not fall, given its division into independent sections and its redundant structural design.

A final characteristic of fracture-critical systems lies in their sensitivity to exponential stress on any one part. Had inspectors attached strain gauges to the gusset plates of the i-35w bridge before it collapsed, they would have seen a gradual increase in stress on the plates, with a rapid rise in the strain on them just before the plates fractured and the bridge fell. That sudden, exponential increase in the strain in a structure prior to failure is a well-known phenomenon, but a fracture-critical design magnifies its effect. What may seem like a contained or controllable problem in one element can quickly become catastrophic because of the peculiar nature of exponential growth, doubling with each increment of time. The danger of such exponential growth lies not only in the system itself, with its rapidly accelerating stress, but also in our own thinking that we have plenty of time and adequate reserves in such situations—just before the window of opportunity to respond can swiftly close.

To understand how these characteristics of redundancy, connectedness, efficiency, and exponential change relate to each other, look at the concept of panarchy, explored in a book by that name edited by the ecologists Lance Gunderson and C. S. Holling.[5] Panarchy describes the way in which human and natural systems move in continuous adaptive cycles, where exponential growth in the connectedness and efficiency within a system eventually makes it less and less resilient, leading eventually to its collapse back to a state of greater resilience, with fewer connections and less efficiency. Fracture-critical designs like the i-35w bridge represent the height of connectedness and efficiency, with the least amount of resiliency, and their collapse tells us, if we understand this as an adaptive cycle, that we need to replace them with systems that have greater resilience and less connectedness and efficiency.

Fracture-Critical Culture

The fracture-critical structures we started to put in place in the 1950s and 1960s represented the larger culture at the time. In 1958, the economist John Kenneth Galbraith noted in his book *The Affluent Society* that ours had become a nation after World War II that accepted "private affluence" and "public squalor" as the norm. In such a cultural milieu, investment in public infrastructure could not keep up with the rapid increase in private wealth in this country.[6] That, in turn, put designers and their governmental clients under increasing pressure to do as much as they could as efficiently as possible, given the relative lack of money available for all that we wanted done. The paradox here is that, at the very moment America could have afforded the very best infrastructure in the world, we decided instead to direct far more wealth into private hands and to begin to squeeze the public realm of funds. The elimination of redundancy and the dramatic increase in the interconnectedness and efficiency in our infrastructure became one of the ways in which we managed this paradox, as engineers and their clients tried to get as much capacity for as little investment as possible.

A broader shift in American culture probably had some effect as well. As many commentators and critics have observed, the United States emerged from World War II not only as the leading economic and military power in the world but also as a nation with a great deal of hubris, the excessive pride and arrogance that, as ancient Greek dramatists knew, can lead to the downfall of those who have the most to gain as well as the most to lose.[7] We now know, of course, that our enemies as well as our allies in the Second World War have proven to be very good competitors and that we can no longer take our dominant position since 1945 for granted. But in the decades immediately following the war, the elimination of redundancy and the pursuit of efficiency in our infrastructure expressed an overconfidence in our technological prowess that the winning of World War II seemed to instill.

The I-35W bridge stands, then, not just as a physical structure over the Mississippi River but also as a political, economic, and social symbol of postwar America. Its fracture-critical design represents all of the systems that we put in place after World War II that have a similar vulnerability to sudden and complete failure because of the elimination of redundancy, and its collapse serves as a warning of future catastrophic events that may occur in the many fracture-critical systems that we have come to depend on for much of our health and well-being. The I-35w bridge, in other words, is both a metaphor and an omen, and we would do well to see it as such if we are to avoid even more devastating fracture-critical failures in coming decades.

Our Fracture-Critical Financial System

An example of the failures we may face in the future has been the collapse of what turned out to be a fracture-critical global financial system. We tend not to see global finance as a designed system, but when we look back at the financial collapse of 2008, we can see that it happened in ways very similar to what caused the I-35w bridge to fail. Just as the failure of one set of gusset plates brought that entire bridge down, so too did the failure of Bear Stearns in March 2008 and then Lehman Brothers and other investment banks and insurance companies starting in September 2008 set off a chain-reaction collapse of the credit and stock markets around the world. Just as the highway crews piled on extra weight while resurfacing the I-35w roadway before the bridge went down, so too did the markets pile huge amounts of debt onto the financial system, overloading banks to the point of collapse. And just as government inspectors and consultants did not catch the problem of deflecting gusset plates on the I-35w bridge or understand the risk involved in not reinforcing them before they failed, government regulators and independent auditors did not provide enough oversight or have adequate understanding of what a loss of confidence in mortgage-backed securities in one part of the financial system could have on the rest.

Once we see the collapse of our fracture-critical financial system as an adaptive cycle, we can begin to predict what will follow and what we will need to do in order to prevent this from happening again. Our global banking system will likely emerge from the current crisis less connected, less efficient, and more resilient than it was. As in a resilient bridge, a transformed financial system will need to have more discrete, disconnected parts, with strong divisions among them so that even if one aspect of the system fails, the rest would be insulated from possible collapse. It will also need to have more redundant parts, with more checks and balances to ensure that if someone makes a calculation error or even a conscious effort to subvert the system, inspectors would catch it before it could bring the entire structure down. Finally, it will lack the speed and efficiency of the fracture-critical system that preceded it. Transactions might have delays built into them, allowing for extra time and added review in order to ensure that the movement of funds is intentional and not improper. Indeed, the very idea of a globally integrated financial system might itself disappear, as nations hurt by the previous collapse over which they had almost no control might set up their own review procedures and regulatory policies to make sure that a worldwide melt-down would not so adversely affect them in the future.

The global scope of the financial meltdown highlights the importance of spotting these potential failures before they occur. It was bad enough for over 150 people to die or be injured as a result of the I-35w bridge's failure. Seeing the financial losses and negative impact on the lives of millions of people around the world as a result of the financial collapse, leading to a rapid slowdown in the global economy and the bankruptcy of many businesses and individuals, should lead us to make the identification of fracture-critical systems one of our top priorities. Even if we cannot prevent the return of a system on an adaptive cycle back to a state of greater resiliency, we can prepare people and lessen the blow, especially to those who are most vulnerable.

This, in turn, suggests a new role for design. We typically train designers—engineers, architects, and planners—to deal primarily with our physical infrastructure, our roads and bridges, buildings and landscapes, cities and regions. The financial collapse suggests that we need to expand that skill set to include nonphysical systems whose operation has all of the characteristics of physical infrastructure but whose design, in the hands of nondesigners, has led to the problems we now face. Those who designed the subprime mortgage systems clearly lacked the skill that all designers learn in anticipating alternative future scenarios in order to assess the potential vulnerabilities and points of failure in a system before it becomes a reality. That ability to look ahead and scope out possible fracture-critical collapses has become extraordinarily valuable and something that the design community has to offer the larger decision-making world. As Roger Martin, dean of the Rotman School of Management at the University of Toronto, has said, companies need designers not only to devise innovative products for the marketplace but also to develop creative—and, I would add, resilient—strategies in the board room.[8]

Our Fracture-Critical Flood Walls

Once we understand the nature of fracture-critical design, we begin to see its prevalence in many of the systems we depend on and how devastating their collapse can be for large numbers of people. Consider New Orleans' fracture-critical levee system. While Hurricane Katrina certainly stressed that system with high winds and waves, the flooding of the city came after the hurricane had begun to subside and the weakened levees gave way in a few places, inundating the city with polluted water. The levee system in New Orleans had fracture-critical features.

If the levee broke at any point around New Orleans, there was no redundant layer of levee walls and no alternative route for the water to go until the break could be repaired. The city depended entirely on the efficient and highly interconnected levees to stand, with pumps as the main backup should water overtop the walls—a backup clearly incapable of handling the floodwaters once the levees failed. At the same time, the connectedness of all parts of the city created a condition in which a levee break at any point led to the inundation of neighborhoods far from the breach.

A more resilient design of the city would have had features with a lot of redundancy both in the design of the primary levees as well as in the design of the city, with redundant barriers among neighborhoods to ensure that the flooding from a break in the wall would remain localized. A more resilient design would also have been designed to handle the worst possible situation—not the average hurricane or flood surge, but the worst imaginable. Of course, it takes more money to design a system this way, but it would cost far, far less than the alternative of hundreds of millions of dollars of property damage and personal loss.

The Dutch certainly understand the cost benefit. Like New Orleans, much of Holland stands below sea level, and it, too, struggles to ensure the stability of its system of dikes. But unlike the levees around New Orleans, in which one break led to the flooding of large parts of the city, the Dutch divide their land into small *polders*—some three thousand in all—so that if a dike fails, the flood damage remains minimal, avoiding the catastrophic failure of a fracture-critical system, as happened in New Orleans.[9] The Dutch also use local materials in the construction of many of their dikes, allowing for continual repair if signs of weakening occur and minimizing the cost of such repair when needed. That resiliency also contrasts with the large-scale and high-cost repair and maintenance requirements of the New Orleans system, whose very expense led to the deferred maintenance that ultimately contributed to the levee's failure. The irony of fracture-critical systems, often justified because of their efficient use of materials and lower initial cost, is that they cost more money over time in repair and maintenance and in the extreme costliness of repairing or replacing the system if it fails.

The Dutch levees suggest some principles that we would do well to learn as we face the task of designing a more resilient infrastructure for ourselves. First, we need to reduce the scale and increase the diversity of the systems on which we depend. This runs counter to the idea that has driven our infrastructure for the last century, which focused on centrally controlled, national-scale systems such as the levees along our rivers put in place by the u.s. Army Corps of Engineers. We have tended to see strength in uniformity and large scale, when in fact such systems—unless they have incredible redundancy—end up also causing uniform, large-scale damage when they fail. The more diverse the system and the smaller the scale, the less likely any one failure will endanger more than a few people or prove too costly to repair, as the Dutch have learned. Second, we need to base our systems on local materials and capabilities. This follows from the previous point, since a more locally based infrastructure will, as a matter of course, have more diverse and smaller-scale units. This, too, comes up against the dominant idea of the recent past of using the newest materials and the biggest technology, when in fact the resiliency of a system increases when a community can construct, maintain, and even repair its own infrastructure without having to wait for the newest and biggest to arrive.

A Fracture-Critical Forecast

We may recognize fracture-critical designs after they fail, whether caused by inadequate gusset plates, subprime mortgages, or insufficient levees, but what about those that have yet to collapse? What are they, where are they, and how can we prevent—or at least mitigate—their failure? As it happens, most fracture-critical systems give us warning signs before they go. The gusset plates on the I-35W bridge had begun to bend long before they broke, and bridge inspectors had even taken photographs of them in that deformed state without doing anything about it. Potential fracture-critical failures, in other words, often stare us in the face, and we have only to recognize their signs.

The nation's electrical grid offers one example of this. On August 15, 2003, a local power failure near Cleveland cascaded into the largest power failure in North American history, leaving 50 million people in large portions of the United States and Canada without power for days and causing an estimated $10 billion in damages.[10] Five years after the blackout, industry experts worry that the situation has gotten worse rather than better, with excess capacity in the electrical power grid declining and demand for electricity by 2030 expected to increase 29 percent from 2006 levels. This exemplifies the kind of fracture-critical system we need to attend to immediately. One failure can bring large sections of the system down, affecting a huge number of people and causing damages that cost far more than the expense of adding capacity and building in redundancy and firewalls to contain a failure to a local area. In an era of terrorism, in which a few people look for opportunities to create the most chaos and alarm as easily as possible, our fracture-critical electrical grid lends itself to sabotage, making the added cost of a more resilient system an even better investment.

Still, the electrical grid, as a fracture-critical design that has yet to collapse, remains relatively easy to see because it constitutes a single, nationwide system. Harder to spot are those failing structures that don't seem connected or even related, such as the many suburban housing developments we have constructed since World War II. Before the war, and indeed through most of American history, we built communities over time, composed of a variety of building types with a mix of uses and a range of housing sizes for a number of different individuals and families. Such varied communities in the past generated a high degree of resiliency because of their social and economic diversity. Since the Second World War, however, we have put in place suburban developments characterized by single uses, often with structures having very similar sizes and price points and mostly built at the same time by the same contractor. Developers found such uniformity easier to finance, build, market, and sell, with the promise to prospective homeowners that their neighbors would be much like them and that they would not have to worry about possible conflicts or nuisances that can occur in more compact, mixed-use and mixed-income communities.[11]

Like the rest of the infrastructure we began installing in the postwar period, these suburban developments have also proven to have a fracture-critical nature. When homeowners default on their mortgage and get foreclosed on, a bank will typically lower the price of the house in order to sell quickly to recoup some of the loss. But if enough foreclosures occur in a development in which the other houses have essentially the same design, the value of all the properties begins to fall, to the point where many homeowners find themselves "underwater," paying more for their mortgages than their houses are worth.[12] This, in turn, creates an incentive for more homeowners to walk away and more banks to foreclose, which creates a downward spiral that can lead to the economic collapse of the entire neighborhood. As with the I-35w bridge, a few cracks in the market value of a homogeneous community and the whole thing can come crashing down.

We have also started to recognize the fracture-critical quality in our oil-dependent transportation system, whose failure would prove devastating to our economy. While we have known about our vulnerability to a sudden cut-off of our excessive demand for oil, more than half of which comes from foreign sources, we continue to depend on oil as the major energy source for our transportation system and seem content with it every time the market price for oil goes down.[13] While working on alternative fuels makes sense and should continue as rapidly as possible, the larger problem lies in our dependence on any one source for most of our transportation needs. Even an alternative source like biofuel, if it becomes too dominant, can lead to all sorts of unintended negative consequences, as we discovered with the impact that large-scale production of ethanol has on water supplies and the price of food.

The only resilient path involves a wide range of alternative sources of energy—not just oil and biofuel but electricity and hydrogen as well as solar, wind, and even human pedal or pedestrian power. Visitors to India often remark at the diversity of transportation modes on many of its streets, from cars and trucks to mopeds and rickshaws to bikes and cows. In the past we might have considered this backward, a holdover from earlier centuries that we moderns had long ago left behind, but the diversity of transportation in India is precisely what the rest of the world needs so that if one source of energy fails, there are many more able to take its place.

Fracture-Critical Fatalities

The extraordinary number of fracture-critical systems put in place in the last century makes it hard to know which to tackle first. Should we repair all of the fracture-critical bridges, redesign our fracture-critical financial system, reinforce our fracture-critical levees, or add

diversity and redundancy to our electrical grid, housing developments, or transportation system? The answer, of course, is all of the
above, since the sudden collapse of any one of these could lead to economic disruption to a devastating degree. Despite that, these may not
be the most important systems to focus on right away. There are phe-
nomena experiencing exponential increases that could produce not
just economic disruption but the potential collapse of our civilization, and we have an obligation to attend to them first.

Jared Diamond, in his book *Collapse*, estimates that we have about
fifty years before we see the effects of the exponential declines in natural habitats, fish populations, biological diversity, and farmable soil;
before we reach a ceiling on inexpensive fossil fuels, accessible fresh
water, and plant growth per acre; and before we see the effects of
exponential increases in toxic chemicals in the air and water, invasive plant species devastating ecosystems, ozone-depleting atmospheric gases, impoverished human populations, and unsustainable
levels of consumption. Diamond argues that we need to attend to all
of the items on this list if we are to avoid a collapse of civilization, at
least as we have known it, although some of the challenges he iden-
tifies should worry us more than others.[14]

We can, for example, learn to live without readily available oil
or without the levels of consumption that have become common in
countries like the United States over the last fifty years. But exponential increases in toxic chemicals, atmospheric gases, and human
population, combined with a decline in farmable soil and a ceiling
on fresh water and plant growth per acre, represent a fatal mix for
us. It is one thing to watch financial institutions collapse and quite
another to see human populations do so as the result of disease or
starvation in a population that had grown too rapidly. Allowing our
numbers to rise exponentially, from 2 billion to an estimated 9 billion people in the hundred years between 1950 and 2050, may be close
to suicidal for us unless we aggressively change the way in which
we inhabit the planet: dramatically reducing the toxins we manufac-
ture, the carbon we emit, the habitat we destroy, the fresh water we
use, and the amount and type of food we consume. The alternative—

a massive die-off of human beings—is the kind of collapse that we must do absolutely everything we can to avoid.

A More Resilient Future

We need to recognize, in other words, that our species itself has become fracture-critical. As we have been destroying the habitat for so many other species, rendering them extinct at rates never before seen during human history, we have also been overstressing the natural systems on which we, ourselves, depend for our survival. Most of us don't recognize the danger we are in, any more than those driving over or working on the I-35w bridge recognized the danger they were in seconds before it fell. Indeed, the apparent strength and invincibility of the systems and structures we have designed to support our civilization can blind us to our vulnerability, as the sheer size and scale of the I-35w bridge seemed to blind its inspectors of its liability to sudden collapse. But, as happened with that bridge, so too with our civilization: the higher and mightier we have become, the farther and faster we can fall.

We don't have to look far to envision a less fracture-critical future for ourselves. Humans have long lived in more resilient and sustainable ways, husbanding finite resources to ensure that future generations have enough, cultivating renewable resources to maintain their quantity and diversity, allocating desirable resources in ways that prevent overconsumption, and encouraging the enjoyment of infinite resources such as human community, creativity, and empathy. In material terms, this means a radical reduction in the quantity of the things we have, the spaces we inhabit, and the distances we travel. Like most of our ancestors, whose physical environment remained extremely modest and constrained in comparison to modern life, we will need to return to living within our environmental means as a species, which will be considerably less than generations in our recent past, given the greatly increased numbers of us on the planet.

That will not be easy for those of us who measure progress in terms of our profligacy. To them, the reduced quantities in our lives will seem like loss, and no doubt many people who have prospered from our domination of the planet will do all they can to resist any change, but we cannot let their fear dissuade us from doing what we need to do in order to preserve ourselves and to survive. If we can get past the hurdle of fear and resistance, we will find that the past gives us plenty of precedents from which to choose. Human societies and settlements have proven most resilient—and least fracture-critical—when they have lived in units small enough to induce a sense of each member's responsibility for each other while remaining relatively autonomous and depending largely on local production and consumption of goods and services.

Building a New Bridge

The structure that replaced the I-35W bridge might also serve as a guide. Unlike its fracture-critical predecessor, the new bridge represents, metaphorically, the kind of change we need to enact in much of the infrastructure we have put in place over the last half century or more. First, the new bridge, designed by Linda Figg of Figg Bridge Engineers, has an extraordinary amount of redundancy built into it.[15] The sheer size and depth of the new bridge's post-tensioned, concrete box beams not only compensate for the weakness of the previous bridge but also demonstrate the realization that it is ultimately better to build well at the beginning than to rebuild at a much greater expense later on, after something has failed. Shortsighted efficiency at the start can lead to extraordinary costs in the end.

Second, the new bridge has great resiliency designed into it. It stands, for example, as essentially two bridges, side by side, without a physical link between the two over the river, so that even if one side would fail for some unlikely reason, the other would remain intact and still functional. Creating disconnected and discrete parts within a system remains one of the best ways to ensure the survivability of the whole. The new bridge will also accommodate multiple modes of transportation, with some lanes strengthened to support future light rail transit and with a pedestrian bridge planned for suspension beneath the highway span. The greater the number of alternatives a system can provide, the greater the likelihood that it will endure.

Finally, the new bridge arose out of local conditions. Those conditions ranged from the specifics of the site, in which the closed-off highway on one end of the bridge became the construction yard for the new structure, to the specific concerns of the community, in which local decision makers and the community at large had opportunities to give extensive input to the bridge's designers. The bridge also involved hundreds of local construction workers and materials suppliers, showing how investment in better infrastructure amounts to one of the best ways to encourage economic activity, not only in the short term through job creation, but also over the long term through higher productivity and greater security within a community.

If the new I-35W bridge indicates what a fracture-resistant infrastructure might be like, it also shows that a more resilient future will look a lot like what we have known in the past. The new bridge, for instance, uses the same material—reinforced concrete—and has a similar mass as the adjacent, eighty-year-old, Tenth Avenue bridge. While the Figg design employs new techniques, like post-tensioning and prefabrication, which hadn't yet been widely developed in 1929, the new I-35W bridge has more in common with the Tenth Avenue bridge than it has to its immediate fracture-critical predecessor.

That will likely be true of most of the infrastructure that we need to build or rebuild in the next fifty years. Our future will look more like our more distant past than the science-fiction fantasies that we have pursued since World War II, resulting in the fracture-critical circumstances that the planet and its people can no longer sustain. Over the coming decades, we need to bring together all of the environmental knowledge we have in order to nurture the natural systems that we depend on, with all of the ethical understanding we can muster to help us thrive within the material constraints we will face. Of the bridges we will need to build in the process, the bridge in understanding that will help us leave behind our old hubris in order to reach a newfound humility may be the most important of all.

NOTES

1. *Minneapolis Star Tribune*, August 2, 2007.

2. "NTSB Determines Inadequate Load Capacity Due to Design Errors of Gusset Plates Caused I-35W Bridge to Collapse," National Transportation Safety Board press release, November 14, 2008, http://www.ntsb.gov/Pressrel/2008/081114.html.

3. "Inspection and Management of Bridges with Fracture-Critical Details," National Cooperative Highway Research Program, a Synthesis of Highway Practice, Transportation Research Board of the National Academies, Synthesis 354, http://www.trb.org/publications/nchrp/nchrp_syn_354.pdf.

4. National Register of Historic Places, Hennepin County, Minnesota, http://www.nationalregisterofhistoricplaces.com/mn/Hennepin/state.html.

5. *Panarchy: Understanding Transformations in Human and Natural Systems*, ed. Lance Gunderson and C. S. Holling (Washington, D.C.: Island Press, 2002).

6. John Kenneth Galbraith, *The Affluent Society* (New York: Houghton Mifflin, 1958).

7. Theodore Draper, "American Hubris, from Truman to the Persian Gulf," *New York Review of Books* 34, no. 12 (July 16, 1987), http://www.nybooks.com/articles/article-preview?article_id=4706.

8. Roger Martin, "At the Crossroads of Design and Business," *Business Week*, July 21, 2006, http://www.rotman.utoronto.ca/rogermartin/publications.htm.

9. "The Scene of Land and Water," http://static.nai.nl/polders/e/index.html.

10. Mark Williams, "5 Years after a Giant Blackout, Concerns about Electrical Grid Linger," Associated Press, August 13, 2008.

11. Andres Duany, Elizabeth Plater-Zyberk, and Jeff Speck, *Suburban Nation: The Rise of Suburban Sprawl and the Decline of the American Dream* (New York: North Point Press, 2000).

12. James R. Hagerty and Ruth Simon, "Housing Pain Gauge: Nearly 1 in 6 Owners 'Under Water': More Defaults and Foreclosures Are Likely as Borrowers with Greater Debt Than Value in Their Homes Are Put in a Tight Spot," *Wall Street Journal*, October 8, 2008, http://online.wsj.com/article/SB122341352084512611.html.

13. James Howard Kuntsler, *The Long Emergency: Surviving the Converging Catastrophes of the Twenty-First Century* (New York: Atlantic Monthly Press, 2005).

14. Jared Diamond, *Collapse: How Societies Choose to Fail or Succeed* (New York: Viking, 2005).

15. FIGG Engineering, *Bridging the Mississippi: The New I-35W Bridge, Minneapolis, Minnesota*, self-published, 2008, http://www.figgbridge.com/new_I35W_bridge_book.html.

CHAPTER TWO

The Infamous Gusset Plates

Roberto Ballarini and Minmao Liao

The general public was shocked and saddened by the practically instantaneous collapse of the I-35W bridge and its tragic consequences. In addition to sharing the emotions experienced by the public, structural engineering experts, including the authors of this essay, were perplexed. What could have caused this very common type of bridge to collapse within a matter of seconds?

The media immediately searched for answers—why did the bridge collapse and who is to blame? Speculative answers to the first question were proposed by average Joes and structural engineering experts alike and involved the usual suspects: the growth from microscopic to catastrophic lengths of undetected cyclic load-induced fatigue cracks, the reduction in strength of steel components produced by environmentally assisted corrosion, and settlement of the piers that transfer the weight of the bridge to the ground. The adequacy of the steel truss design, which was used in the longest span of the bridge, was questioned. It is true that steel trusses possess a relatively small level of redundancy. That is, the integrity of a steel truss bridge can be jeopardized if but a few critical members or connections fail. However, the possibility of such catastrophic events is for all intents and purposes eliminated by mandated regularly conducted maintenance, retrofit, and inspection procedures. As for blame, fingers were first pointed at the deck repair construction that was taking place at the time of the collapse as being the straw that broke the camel's back. This is understandable considering that a few hours before the collapse hundreds of tons of gravel, sand, and water trucks used to repair the concrete deck were placed on the main span.

The collapse was such an unusual and unexpected event that the senior author decided early on that he would not participate in speculation. Instead, he recognized that this atypical catastrophe offered a learning opportunity for undergraduate and graduate students. A few days after the collapse the senior author and his colleague Taichiro Okazaki applied for and obtained financial support from the National Science Foundation for an independent academic investigation. Soon after, the University of Minnesota's Center for Transportation Studies provided supplementary support. The investigative team included Department of Civil Engineering professors Taichiro Okazaki, Ted Galambos, and Arturo Schultz; graduate students Minmao Liao and Alicia Forbes; and undergraduate students Tor Oksnevad and Charles DeVore. This essay summarizes the steps involved in this investigation and explains how a few incorrectly designed gusset plates resulted in the collapse of a bridge that served Minneapolis well for forty years. Further details of the investigation are provided in technical publications by the authors.[1]

The authors note that the scope of their investigation was not as large as those of the official investigations performed by the National Transportation Safety Board (NTSB), the Federal Highway Administration, and the Minnesota Department of Transportation (MN/DOT). A reader interested in a more complete investigation is referred to the final report by the NTSB[2] and a report prepared by Wiss, Janney, Elstner Associates (WJE), Inc., which was commissioned by MN/DOT.[3]

The Mechanics of the Bridge

The main structural components of the bridge and the location of the U10 node that is the focus of this study are highlighted in Figure 2.1A. Traffic was supported by a concrete deck resting on steel

FIGURE 2.1A » Main structural components of the I-35W bridge. Photograph courtesy of John A. Weeks III.

FIGURE 2.1B » Close-up view of the gusset plates at the U10 node, from official report of the National Transportation Safety Board, Office of Research and Engineering, filed March 7, 2008.

beams (referred to as stringers) running along the direction of traffic. The stringers were in turn supported by steel floor trusses, perpendicular to the direction of traffic and distributed along the length of the bridge. The floor trusses were supported by the main trusses. As shown in the image, a truss is a structural system formed as an assembly of triangular units, where each unit is composed of three slender members. Figure 2.1B is an image of a typical node of the main truss, defined as a point where truss members (five in this case) come together. As shown in the image, the truss members in the I-35W bridge were held together by gusset plates riveted on two sides of the members. Ultimately, the weight of the bridge and the traffic was transferred to the ground through concrete piers.

It is very important to note that if the bridge had been designed correctly, the gusset plate connections would have been the strong links and the truss members the weak links in the chain defined by the structure. In other words, failure of the truss members would have preceded failure of the gusset plates in a hypothetical typical collapse.

The bridge underwent repair and a number of modifications during its service life. The reconstructions most significant to the collapse were conducted in 1977 and 1998 and involved increasing the thickness of the concrete deck from 6.5 to 8.5 inches and the addition of new concrete parapets and guard rails. For those not familiar with the relative weights of the components of a bridge of this type, it is noted here that when the bridge was first opened for traffic, the concrete deck comprised 70 percent of the total bridge weight (the fact that the weight of the concrete deck is much larger than all of the steel that makes up the bridge is not obvious from the image shown in Figure 2.1A). Therefore, the concrete added in later years increased the weight of the bridge by more than 20 percent and thus represented a significant increase in the demand on the structural components. In terms of a mental image, the addition of 2.0 inches of concrete to the deck was equivalent to doubling the weight of the steel.

The first step in the investigation, performed by Tor Oksnevad and Charles DeVore, involved the translation of a large volume of design drawings into the computerized structural analysis model of the bridge shown in Figure 2.2A. The structural analysis model is

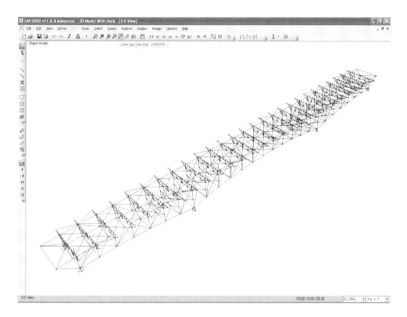

FIGURE 2.2A » Computer structural analysis model of the main span of the bridge. Authors' photograph.

FIGURE 2.2B » Detailed finite element (computer) model of the U10 node. Authors' photograph.

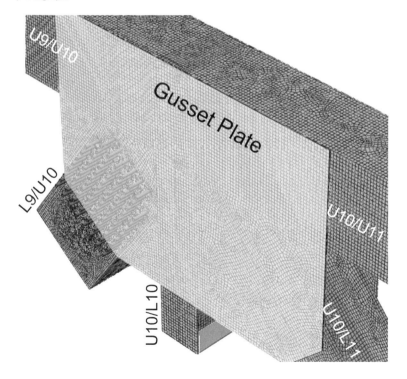

referred to as a global model because it includes the main structural components described previously through Figure 2.1A but not the finest details of the bridge such as the gusseted connections. At the end of summer 2007, the undergraduate students handed off this mathematical representation of the bridge to Alicia Forbes and Minmao Liao, who used it to calculate the forces produced in all of the main structural components of the bridge in response to different types of loads, including the self-weight of the bridge, the traffic, and the construction material present on the day of the collapse.

The forces calculated using the structural analysis model were applied by Minmao Liao to a refined model, as shown in Figure 2.2B, of the connection referred to on the design drawings as node U10 and also indicated in Figure 2.1A. This connection involves the infamous gusset plates whose failure we determined to have initiated the bridge collapse. The detailed model is referred to as a finite element model because the connection is represented by a very large but finite number of much smaller volume elements. The mechanical behavior of the connection was determined by solving a very large system of equations obtained by assembling the equations of each volume element on the supercomputer housed at the Minnesota Supercomputer Institute.

Elasticity versus Plasticity

The explanation of why the gusset plate at U10 failed requires an understanding of the concepts of elasticity, plasticity, and the structural design guidelines that were in place when the bridge was built. The simple demonstration involving the bending of a partially uncoiled metallic paper clip, captured in the images shown in Figure 2.3, illustrates the difference between elastic and plastic behaviors. As the coiled portion of the clip is held tight, pushing the far end of the straight portion produces a deformation that is associated with a rotation about the hinge point labeled H. The top three images show that when a relatively small displacement is applied and then removed, the straight portion of the clip springs back to its original position. However, if the applied displacement is larger than a critical amount, then the straight portion does not return to its original configuration after removal of the force. Instead it exhibits a permanent deformation, which is a result of damage of the material in the vicinity of hinge *H*. This damage is referred to as plastic deformation, and it can result in fracture of the paper clip. One way that plastic damage can lead to failure of the paper clip is referred to as plastic collapse and involves increasing the rotation about the hinge to a point that breaks the paper clip into two pieces. Another way is through so-called low-cycle fatigue, whereby the clip is subjected to repetitive cycles of counterclockwise followed by clockwise rotations about the hinge.

When the bridge was built, the design code reflected the philosophy that no component of the bridge should be allowed to experience potentially dangerous plastic deformation. This design paradigm is referred to as allowable stress design, and it demands (and if performed correctly guarantees) that all components will remain elastic under service conditions. The design code also prescribes a safety factor of approximately 2.0 to each structural component, which means that the gusset plates should be designed to remain elastic even if they are subjected to forces twice those expected.

As explained through the computer analyses described in the next section, for some unknown reason the gusset plates at node U10 were designed incorrectly. In order for them to have remained elastic with an acceptable factor of safety, the design procedures available when the bridge was designed called for the gusset plates at U10 to be 1.0 inch thick. Instead they were 0.5 inch thick. The results of our analyses showed that the elastic safety fac-

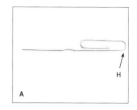

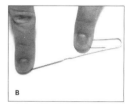

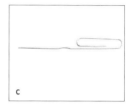

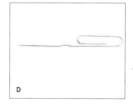

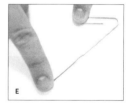

FIGURE 2.3 » Demonstration of elasticity *(A–C)* and plasticity *(D–F)*. Authors' photographs.

FIGURE 2.4 » U10 node after bridge collapse, from official report of the National Transportation Safety Board, Office of Research and Engineering, filed March 7, 2008.

tor of the gusset plates as they were constructed was approximately equal to 1.0 instead of 2.0. In other words, addition of forces beyond those in the original design could introduce dangerous plastic deformation into the gusset plates.

Computer Simulation of Plastic Deformation in Gusset Plates at U10

Through computer simulations we were able to demonstrate that just prior to the collapse the demand on the gusset plates at node U10 was essentially equal to their capacity.

A few days after the collapse, the NTSB and MN/DOT allowed the authors to visit the site of the bridge collapse. What immediately appeared strange was the fact that some of the connections failed, even though (as mentioned previously) they are supposed to be the strong links in the chain defined by the bridge. The postcollapse image shown in Figure 2.4 suggests that failure of the connection at node U10 was associated with separation between the chord truss member U9/U10W and the diagonal truss member L9/U10W.

A finite element model of the U10 connection that includes the detailed geometry of the truss members, the gusset plates, and the rivet holes is shown in Figure 2.2B. Figure 2.5 presents simplified schematics of the detailed model of the U10 node that show the extent of plastic deformation experienced by the gusset plates as a result of the forces produced by various loadings as calculated by the global structural analysis model. In these drawings the plastic deformation within the gusset plates is shown in black. One should remember that if the gusset plates had been designed correctly, the occurrence of plastic deformation inside the plate would be limited to extremely small regions in the vicinity of sharp geometric discontinuities.

Figure 2.5A shows that the original weight of the bridge produced forces in the member's framing into node U10 in the range of 1,586 kips tension to 1,713 kips compression (1 kip equals 1,000 pounds) and that these forces introduced plastic deformation within a small volume within the gusset plate. The condition of the gusset plate is not particularly discernable at this stage.

The addition of two inches of concrete deck increased the forces in the members by almost 30 percent, and as shown in Figure 2.5B this increase extended the plastic deformation across the gusset plate along the top chord. The extent of plastic deformation is beyond what is permitted in allowable stress design. More precisely, these results imply that the elastic safety factor of the gusset plates at U10 was barely 1.0, while the allowable stress design requires a safety factor of 2.0.

Figure 2.5C shows the condition produced by the added weight on

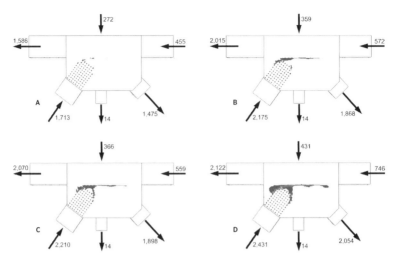

FIGURE 2.5 » Plastic deformation in gusset plates at U10 resulting from *(A)* the weight of the bridge at the time of original construction, including all steel and concrete; *(B)* the addition of two inches of concrete deck in 1977 and 1998; *(C)* the weight of traffic added; *(D)* the weight of construction material and equipment added. All forces have units of kips (1,000 pounds). Authors' photographs.

the day of the bridge collapse. Due to traffic lane closures, the traffic weight was rather light. However, because the gusset plates were substantially yielded under the self-weight of the bridge and the additional concrete, as seen in Figure 2.5B, even that small load addition produced a noticeable extension of plastic deformation. The reason why the extent of plastic deformation increases disproportionately with respect to increased force is because the stiffness of a plasticized steel component is greatly reduced as compared to its elastic stiffness.

The computationally predicted condition of the connection at the instant of bridge collapse is shown in Figure 2.5D. All load effects, including the self-weight of the bridge, traffic weight, and construction material and equipment placed on the day of the bridge collapse, are accounted for. The figure implies that a very substantial portion of the gusset plate was yielded. It is also noted that the pattern of plastic deformation suggests that the gusset plate is approaching a failure corresponding to separations between the horizontal U9/U10W chord and the L9/U10W diagonal, and across the rivet holes on the

L9/U10W diagonal. The predicted failure scenario is consistent with the observed failure shown in Figure 2.4.

The plot in Figure 2.6 shows the computed relationship between the compression in the diagonal truss member L9/U10W and contraction of the selected gauge *L*. Two curves are shown, one for the actual U10 gusset plate and another for a hypothetical gusset plate that is identical to the U10 gusset plate but is one inch thick. The four dotted horizontal lines indicate the force levels corresponding to the four stages shown in Figure 2.5. As the compression was increased from 1,713 kips to 2,431 kips, the response of the half-inch gusset plate softened. The softening is due to the extension of plastic deformation shown in Figure 2.5. The curve indicates that the half-inch-thick gusset plate was approaching its capacity limit where the compression in member L9/U10W cannot be increased any further. The capacity

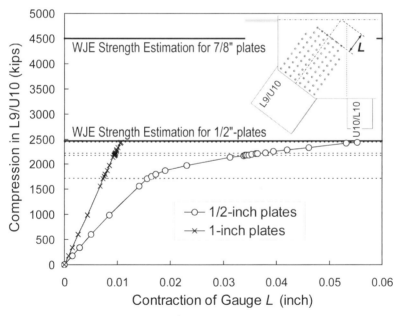

FIGURE 2.6 » Plot of force in the L9/U10W diagonal versus the compression of a selected gauge length at the U10 node, as predicted by the finite element model for the half-inch-thick gusset plate and for a one-inch-thick gusset plate. Also shown on the figure: the capacity of the gusset plates at U10 predicted by the finite element model of WJE and the capacity that would have been achieved by a seven-eighths-inch-thick gusset plate. Authors' photographs.

limit indicates failure of the gusset plate. Meanwhile, the one-inch-thick gusset plate remains elastic under the forces experienced the day of the collapse; it does not exhibit similar softening behavior. Therefore, Figure 2.6 indicates that had the U10 gusset plates been one inch thick instead of one-half inch thick, the tragic bridge collapse would not have happened. We note that the results of this investigation are consistent with those obtained using similar computer modeling by NTSB and WJE. As shown in Figure 2.6, WJE's prediction of the capacity of the half-inch gusset plates is practically the same as the capacity predicted by the authors. This figure also shows that WJE predicted that seven-eighths-inch-thick gusset plates would have had sufficient capacity to resist the forces that existed prior to the collapse.

Conclusions

The results of our academic investigation can be summarized as follows:

1. It was determined using a computerized structural analysis of the I-35W bridge that the members of the main truss had acceptable safety factors when they were designed. The capacity of the truss members was larger than the demands placed on them throughout the life of the bridge, including those on the day of the collapse. While many truss members fractured when they fell to the ground, we are not aware of any evidence that indicates that failure of a truss member initiated the collapse.

2. With respect to the design service loads, the elastic safety factor of the gusset plates at nodes U10 was approximately equal to 1.0, instead of approximately 2.0 as required by the design code in 1967. For some unknown reason, these gusset plates were one-half inch instead of one inch thick.

3. The bridge collapsed as a result of the failure of the gusset plate(s) at a U10 node, in the vicinity of the L9/U10 compression diagonal. These plates experienced extensive plastic deformation. The calculated capacity of the gusset plates

that failed was very close to the demands that were placed on them at the time of the collapse. Had the plates been one inch thick, their capacity would have exceeded the demand placed on them, and they would not have experienced any plastic deformation.

4. Temperature cycles could have significantly influenced the forces in the truss members framing into the U10 nodes and in the stresses experienced by the gusset plates, as could have a number of heavy vehicles passing over the bridge near the time of collapse.

5. The final straw was most likely the weight of the construction material placed on the bridge hours before the collapse. The calculations show that the addition of this weight produced a very large region of plastic deformation in the gusset plates and rendered a demand on the gusset plates that for all intents and purposes was equal to their capacity.

One of the authors (RB) was recently asked what could be learned from the collapse of the I-35W bridge. His response: "The Devil is in the details."

NOTES

1. M. Liao, T. Okazaki, R. Ballarini, A. E. Schultz, and T. V. Galambos, "Analysis of Critical Gusset Plates in the Collapsed I-35W Bridge," paper presented at the 2009 Structures Congress, ASCE, Austin, Texas, April 30–May 2, 2009.

2. *Collapse of I-35W Highway Bridge, Highway Accident Report*, NTSB/HAR-08/03, November 14, 2008.

3. *I-35W Bridge over the Mississippi River: Collapse Investigation*, Final Report, November 2008, WJE No. 2007-3702, Wiss, Janney, Elstner Associates, Inc.

CHAPTER THREE

Building the New Bridge: Process and Politics in City-Building

Patrick Nunnally

Two weeks after the August 1, 2007, collapse of the I-35W bridge, I met with colleagues who were part of the University's new Mississippi River Initiative. We had begun to develop programs that explored ways to better connect the University's research, teaching, and civic engagement efforts to the river that runs through the heart of the Minneapolis campus. The bridge collapse and recovery efforts had put the river, albeit as the scene of a tragedy, on the front page of newspapers across the country. Would it be possible, we wondered, to pull together a course on this disaster and what happened in its aftermath? Could we do so in a way that was respectful to victims and their families and that stayed clear of the political rumblings that were already starting to be heard?

I was selected to put the course together. Together, we all contributed ideas and funding support from our various departments and centers, and we all collaborated to make the course a reality. A mere month after the disaster, the new "Special Topics in Urban Studies" course was ready to be offered for undergraduate credit. The building of the new bridge began parallel with the class, and the class tracked it closely during the fall semester. The replacement bridge opened a year later, in September 2008.

The focus of the course, and of this chapter, is on the urban design and planning issues raised by the new bridge, as well as some salient facts and concepts presented by the bridge itself. We did not feel equipped then, and I do not feel competent now, to go into the dramatic stories of the victims and their experiences after the crash. People interested in these issues might want to consult online news archives, particularly those of Minnesota Public Radio and the *Star Tribune* (Minneapolis–St. Paul). Nor was our focus on the political dimension of the aftermath, although we necessarily touched on it as that became one of the dominant narratives. First responders were heroic, the incident command team put together by the City of Minneapolis ran superbly, and, for about a week, the Democratic mayor of Minneapolis and the Republican state governor were on the same page.

We asked students to consider what "river story" they would tell about this place in five or ten years. If the bridge collapse can be likened to having a hole punched in the fabric of the city, how was the tear being repaired, and what could we learn from that process? That was and remains the subject of ongoing teaching and research at the University. Taken as a whole, the story of the building of the new bridge reveals some new directions in rebuilding civic infrastructure, although the problems and difficulties attendant to this case do not necessarily bode well for our future. A new bridge was built, true, and it is elegant and certainly a stronger, state-of-the-art structure. But the squabbling that led *Star Tribune* columnist Nick Coleman to write that the public discussion about the new bridge was about short-term politics rather than long-term policy tells us that we have a long way to go before we have developed an appropriate process for confronting the issue of aging infrastructure: "The bridge collapse is now almost completely a fight over the spin, not the spans."[1] This chapter takes up the sequence of key decisions that developed a process for repairing a hole in the heart of the physical and emotional city. It addresses almost exclusively the questions arising from the rebuilding of the physical bridge.

I'll address the issue of politics first, because political considerations endured far longer than my students and I thought they would. The fall of 2007 was a time ripe with political drama, as the run-up to the 2008 presidential campaign was beginning to hit its stride. Two local factors increased the visibility of the political dimension of the collapse: Minnesota Governor Tim Pawlenty was chairing the presidential election campaign of Arizona Senator John McCain, and the Republican National Convention was scheduled to open in St. Paul (ten miles downstream from the collapse site and the other city of the Twin Cities) in September 2008. As the rebuilding process unfolded, cynics, and there were plenty of all political persuasions around, suggested that the Minnesota Department of Transportation (MN/DOT) was hurrying the whole process in order to have the success of a completed project ready for the national media who would be visiting in the fall of 2008.

But there were deeper political issues at work also. To be fair, the political sniping did not begin immediately after the collapse. Senator Amy Klobuchar's comment that "in America, a bridge should not simply fall down" was taken as a cry of bewilderment, a lament that something was seriously wrong that would need to be fixed. For the first week or so after the collapse, while victims were still not recovered from the river or were still in critical hospital care, political tensions were muted. Even Pawlenty's rival, Minneapolis's DFL mayor R. T. Rybak, appeared with the governor in a joint appeal for calm and to give thanks to everyone who had worked together so skillfully to manage the emergency of the collapse.

The political truce did not last long. There were pointed questions about why the bridge had collapsed. Pawlenty, who had first been elected in 2002 after making a "no tax increase" pledge and had held firm despite legislative opposition and big state budget cuts, was an easy target. People speculated that his state department of transportation, headed by Lieutenant Governor Carol Molnau, must not have inspected the bridge closely enough, or put sufficient repairs into it, to keep the disaster from happening. Ironically or not, the bridge was under reconstruction at the time of the collapse. Still,

Democratic Congressman James Oberstar, head of the House Transportation Committee, led inquiries into whether infrastructure repairs and maintenance had received the attention they deserved, in Minnesota and across the country. Several analysts called for a thorough public debate over the state of the nation's infrastructure: were other bridges at risk of sudden collapse? Weeks after the disaster, when preliminary results by the National Transportation Safety Board indicated a design flaw might have been part of the problem, the NTSB took the unusual step of releasing the preliminary result in part so that states and counties could examine their inventory of similar bridges and make any necessary immediate corrections in the name of public safety. Nevertheless, national debate about the amount, and target, of public spending on transportation raged for months. Despite the clamor, only one highly visible public official was politically damaged in the year after the collapse. Transportation Commissioner Molnau was refused confirmation by the state senate when it convened in spring 2008 and was therefore forced to relinquish her appointment, although she kept her elected title of lieutenant governor.

Local Economic Impact Drives a Swift Rebuilding Project

From the beginning of MN/DOT's response to the collapse, speed was of the essence, and there was not, apparently, any thought of *not* rebuilding or of exploring alternative modes of transportation. For the first few days after the collapse, public attention was riveted first by the rescue efforts and later by the sad task of recovering the bodies of those who lost their lives. It was not until about a week after the collapse that anyone publicly began to pay close attention to the "now what?" question.

But MN/DOT staff had been hard at work, beginning the morning after the disaster. Environmental review staff began pulling together a plan for emergency compliance reviews the next morning. Traffic managers were faced with the question of what to do with the estimated 140,000 vehicles per day that had used the collapsed bridge, and very quickly came up with a list of projects that would alleviate, although not completely relieve, this traffic. Meanwhile, planners from MN/DOT and the state Department of Employment and Economic Development were calculating how much the collapse of a major metropolitan linkage was costing the region. Working with private econometric consultants, state analysts factored in longer travel times and increased wear and tear on commercial heavy trucks (an estimated five thousand of which had used the bridge daily), as well as higher operating costs to all users arising from longer commutes. The estimated loss to the Minnesota economy from the bridge collapse was $17 million in 2007 and $43 million in 2008. The figure commonly cited for economic impact was $400,000 per day. This figure was to play a major role in subsequent planning for the new bridge.

Need for Swift Rebuild Drives Decision to Design-Build

MN/DOT administrators decided within a week of the collapse to rebuild the bridge and with all speed possible. By August 4, they had begun to reassign staff to the new project and had decided to pursue it as a "design-build" project. As subsequently explained on Web sites and in the press, a design-build project was a variance from the traditional design-bid-build project, but it was not unprecedented in the state, or even in the metropolitan region.[2] Under a design-build scenario, contractors who are bidding to get the contract to do the job propose how they will approach the work. In the case of a bridge replacement like the I-35W bridge project (now termed the St. Anthony Falls Bridge), MN/DOT would give contractors a series of engineering problems and standards that the new bridge would be required to meet. How the contractors chose to solve the given problems and achieve the set standards was the subject of the bid. For instance, a firm with expertise and experience in steel bridge construction could propose a steel bridge, while another could choose concrete if it felt that was a better way to approach the job. The design-build process utilized the expertise of bridge engineers who had built bridges all over the country or, perhaps, the world. Another advantage was that design-build put the cost pressure on the firm rather than on MN/DOT. If a firm bid a project at a particular price, it was up to the firm to do the job for that price. Finally, a design-build project requires continued close cooperation between state engineers and the contractor's staff to ensure that the project is proceeding according to plan and that the design, which continues after construction has started, is seamlessly integrated into the final product.

What is the traditional design-bid-build process, and why was that not chosen? Traditionally, departmental engineers have designed what is needed for a particular road, culvert, or bridge project down to the last detail, tailoring their specifications to their knowledge of the use of the road in question, projected increases in traffic and loads, and all other relevant factors. With every aspect of a project designed by departmental personnel, there is very little variance in terms of what bidding contractors are bidding on: everyone is playing from the same deck, so to speak. This is a crucial point, for if all necessary specifications are dictated by the department, then bidders compete solely on price. The department, as wise custodians of public funds, typically then award a job to the low bidder because all other factors are necessarily equal by the terms of the contract offering. Such was most certainly not the case with the bidding on the new bridge, and this fact led to one of the largest and most recurrent controversies of the whole process.

The Choice of Flatiron-Manson to Build the New Bridge

On August 23, 2007, a Request for Proposals was issued to four bridge companies who were felt by MN/DOT personnel to be qualified to undertake a bridge project of the scope of the St. Anthony Falls Bridge. An earlier Request for Qualifications had laid out the basic parameters of the project: a ten-lane freeway bridge crossing to be built under a very aggressive time schedule and other project-related expectations. The process for bidding and letting the contract, as stipulated by MN/DOT, required bidders to submit technical proposals separately from project budget and time lines. The proposals would be judged according to quality (50 percent), aesthetics/visual quality (20 percent), enhancements (15 percent), and public outreach/involvement (15 percent).[3]

Controversies about the selection unfolded over the criteria of aesthetics and public outreach. Why, critics such as *St. Paul Pioneer Press* columnist Joe Soucheray wondered, was the public paying for a "pretty" bridge and hiring a public relations firm?[4] One possible reason is the project's location. The bridge crosses the Mississippi River at a point that marks the downstream end of the National Register-listed St. Anthony Falls Historic District.

The falls themselves, located less than a mile from the bridge, would be visible from it, and the bridge would be a major visual component of people visiting the historic district. The district was home to the world's leading complex of flour milling from the 1880s until the 1930s and was the birthplace for such international companies as Pillsbury and General Mills. The recently restored railroad Stone Arch Bridge, a national civil engineering landmark in its own right, also lies close to the new bridge location. Great care had to be taken to design a bridge that met the engineering and safety standards established yet fit into the urban and historical context.

As for the need for public involvement, MN/DOT had taken a black eye when the old bridge fell, and the new bridge was the subject of international news coverage as well as repeated extensive local coverage. It was incumbent on the department to make every reasonable effort to inform and involve the public in the construction of this new bridge over which thousands of people would cross daily and that would provide a highway "front door" into the city of Minneapolis for travelers coming from the north. Besides that, the project was going to cost a lot of money.

Just how much money the project would cost touched off another controversy. When the technical proposals were reviewed by six panelists (representing MN/DOT, the City of Minneapolis, and the Associated General Contractors of Minnesota), the Flatiron-Manson team, with design by FIGG Bridge Design, came out on top with an average score of 91.47 out of a possible score of 100 points. Proposals from C. S. McCrossan (69.51), Walsh/American Bridge (67.88), and Ames/Lunda (55.98) trailed far behind.[5]

The MN/DOT's process for determining apparent best value can

FIGURE 3.1 » Taken from above the University of Minnesota campus, this view illustrates the proximity of the I-35W corridor to the St. Anthony Falls Historic District. The thick, white line in the upper center of the photo is St. Anthony Falls, with the iconic Stone Arch Bridge crossing the river immediately below it. The old I-35W bridge is the next one below, located immediately above the concrete-arched Tenth Avenue Bridge. Image from the Metropolitan Design Center Image Bank. Copyright Regents of the University of Minnesota. All rights reserved. Used with permission.

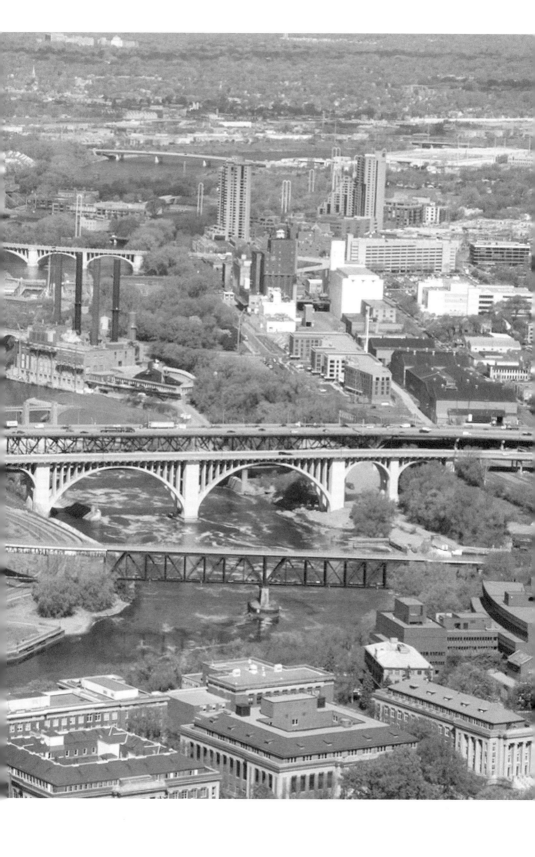

be summarized as cost plus time divided by technical score. Cost and time estimates were opened by a separate team of reviewers after the technical scores had been assessed. Flatiron-Manson's cost estimate, $233 million, was higher than the others, and its estimated time to build the project, 437 days, tied it with the Walsh/American Bridge team. Ames/Lunda had the cheapest proposal at $178 million, while C. S. McCrossan proposed the shortest project time line at 367 days.

For many observers, it defied logic that the most expensive project with the longest time frame would be the best value. But the technical score, on which the Flatiron-Manson bid far outdistanced the others, trumped matters of cost and timing. In other words, rather than buying the cheapest bridge, which could be built in the shortest possible time, MN/DOT, acting through a collaborative, fully audited process, selected the bridge proposal best suited to its needs rather than the cheapest possible. In retrospect, from a perspective after the global economic difficulties that were starting in 2007 and accelerated so spectacularly in 2008, this logic may be questionable. But under the pressures of a collapsed bridge, snarled traffic, neighborhoods and politicians demanding solutions, and public confidence in the department being questioned, the decision makes more sense.

Building a New Bridge in the Heart of the City

Once construction of the St. Anthony Falls Bridge started in late fall of 2007, the project was a more or less constant subject of news coverage in nearly all media. In part, of course, this was because of the MN/DOT-Flatiron strategy of keeping the public fully informed about progress on the new bridge. The project's communications team set up regular e-mail notifications of project status, including notification of traffic and other disruptions that might be felt because of the project's accelerated schedule. Since the construction went on around the clock, it may have been cold comfort to neighbors dealing with the lights at night and the noise of construction to know what to expect, but nevertheless the project team felt that full disclosure was warranted. One of the most popular public information approaches was the institution of regular "Sidewalk Superintendent Talks" led by a senior project engineer every Saturday morning during construction. Sometimes there were several hundred people gathered on the nearby Tenth Avenue Bridge, and there were at least a couple dozen people every Saturday wanting to have someone explain to them what they were seeing.

What they were seeing was, quite possibly, the largest, most intensely developed public construction project in recent Minnesota history. The Flatiron team was offered a large incentive to build the project as quickly as feasible, largely because of the $400,000 per day

FIGURE 3.2 » This illustration from the Minnesota Department of Transportation shows the simultaneous construction of a number of bridge piers and abutments, a condition not normally possible in a bridge reconstruction project. Courtesy of the Minnesota Department of Transportation.

FIGURE 3.3 » This photograph, taken in July 2008 as the bridge spans neared completion, illustrates how multiple work crews were able to work on different parts of the bridge reconstruction project simultaneously. Courtesy of the Minnesota Department of Transportation.

hit the regional economy was taking while the bridge was down. If the bridge could be finished earlier than the stated time line, the Flatiron-Manson contract called for an additional $200,000 per day, half the estimated public cost. In other words, if the bridge opened ten days ahead of schedule, Flatiron-Manson would receive a $2 million bonus. Conversely, if it opened ten days behind schedule, there would be a $2 million penalty. It was felt that the financial incentive structure, coupled with close regular oversight from quality control engineers, would ensure that a high-quality structure would be built in a timely manner.

How could such an enormous project be built so rapidly, yet safely? For one thing, once the site was cleared of debris from the old structure, the construction team had full access to the entire site. This enabled the construction crews to work on both sides of the river simultaneously and to pour concrete for all of the piers at the same time.

Likewise, still other crews could be using other parts of the project site to fabricate the gigantic concrete box girders that would be trucked into place down the nearby West River Parkway before being transported by crane-barge and put into place. Work proceeded around the clock, seven days a week, with some two hundred workers on the job site at nearly all times. This situation is a marked contrast, of course, to a more usual highway bridge replacement, where half the bridge is constructed while traffic continues to use the other half. Ordinary road projects, including bridge replacements, typically have crews on the job for one shift per day, five days a week, as opposed to the accelerated schedule of this project.

But there was more to this process than just building the bridge quickly and keeping the public constantly updated on progress. Two elements of the design process stand out as unusual. The first was the creation of a Visual Quality Team of local stakeholders to advise the MN/DOT-Flatiron team throughout much of the project. Given the project's particular location in a national- and state-designated historic district, representatives from city and state historic preservation agencies were part of this advisory board. The Mississippi River in the Twin Cities is also designated as the Mississippi National River and Recreation Area, a unit of the U.S. National Park Service, so the National Park Service and other river advocates were also part of this team.

There was also a one-day bridge design charette in September 2007 to allow public input on selected aspects of the final design. Elected and appointed officials, plus selected neighborhood and community leaders, participated in a facilitated process to choose the bridge's color, the shape of its piers, and basic configurations of lighting and railings. Many important design issues were off the table of course, but it can be supposed that the details offered for public consideration gave a sense of community ownership to the final product.

A New Bridge Opens: What Have We Learned?
The new I-35W bridge opened to traffic at 5:00 A.M. on Thursday, September 18, 2008, more than three months early. People lined up, some for an hour or more, to be among the first to cross, and by the next day traffic hummed along as if nothing had happened. But of course a lot had happened, and questions and reflections on that process bear some importance. Two items in particular seem salient to issues of city-building.

As discussion about replacing the collapsed bridge began to pick up steam, there had been several voices arguing that MN/DOT should create a "landmark" structure. The architect-engineer Santiago Calatrava was frequently mentioned as a potential designer for such a bridge, and there were several editorials and sharp questions at public meetings about the advisability of taking advantage of this opportunity to build a striking and elegant "entrance" into the city. Upon being questioned by a member of the Minnesota chapter of the American Institute of Architects on this matter, the MN/DOT project manager replied that if Calatrava were a member of one of the proposing teams, his design would certainly get full consideration.

In retrospect, two issues militated against the construction of a landmark or architectural statement bridge. For one, the entire project was on an extremely compressed time line, driven by the economic impact to the region of the collapsed structure. There simply was not time in the process for the kind of consideration, deliberation, and design that would be necessary to create a landmark structure. For another, the location of the construction project, adjacent to the St. Anthony Falls Historic District, was a complicating factor. St. Anthony Falls is one of the spots that can arguably be called the birthplace of Minnesota. The Stone Arch Bridge in the district is becoming an icon of the city as the city's investment in its riverfront is coming to fruition and thousands of people live, work, and attend events in the historic district. The Visual Quality Analysis team took great pains to consider the visual impact of a new bridge on the qualities that define the historic area. Again, it was felt that a dominating, architecturally distinguished landmark would have an adverse impact. This contextualist aesthetic was not universal, though, and even after the bridge design was essentially completed, one could hear laments such as what one of my students said: "Why shouldn't we have a landmark marking our generation and its presence on the river, instead of just celebrating the past?"

The second urban planning and design issue raised by the new bridge was the set of questions about rebuilding the immediate transportation network in the vicinity. Again, the calls for planning and consideration of long-term alternatives fell under the onslaught of the time crunch to replace the lost interstate highway connection, although the new bridge and immediate surroundings do address some pressing neighborhood transportation needs. A number of obsolescent railroad tracks were removed, creating a wider right of way for Second Street Northeast, which might be used for a future bike route connecting the university area to neighborhoods in Northeast Minneapolis. The highway's vertical geometry was improved, so that future replacement of the Fourth Street and University Avenue bridges over the freeway can be achieved with a minimum of future disruption. The central lanes of the bridge in both directions are reinforced sufficiently to carry future light rail transit lines, should the regional rail authorities elect to utilize that route.

But, as is to be expected, I suppose, there are a number of "roads not taken" in this aspect of the project as well. The dominance of cars and trucks as elements of the regional transportation system was never really questioned, leading some to argue that a tremendous opportunity to modernize the region's transportation infrastructure was missed. This lament became particularly telling in the summer of 2008, when the rising price ($4 per gallon) of gasoline was causing people with long commutes to question their transportation choices. Even before the bridge collapse, MN/DOT was working on rebuilding the intersection of I-35W and Washington Avenue, just south of the bridge, which was a frequent bottleneck for traffic leaving the city. "Why not," some wondered, "take advantage of the bridge being out to finally and for all fix the whole interstate/city nexus here, just east of downtown and, at the same time, really make the east side of downtown a nice urban area?" Unfortunately, the federal funding that allowed the bridge to be rebuilt so quickly did not allow for any project creep: only the direct results of the disaster could be alleviated using this emergency funding.

Now, with the bridge opened and memories of the disaster and its aftermath disappearing from the attention of news organizations and most of the public, what do we have and what have we learned? I would suggest half a dozen points to ponder:

- *The bridge itself* is strong, with multiple redundancies against structural failure. Its design is spare and elegant (to my eye, anyway) and MN/DOT has undertaken a program of lighting its underside and piers and abutments at night that makes the structure a dramatic point on the river. It is a "smart bridge," which means that a system of internal monitors respond to traffic flow and generate messages for travelers, control the automatic de-icing system, and send a continuous stream of structural measures to monitors at MN/DOT and in the Civil Engineering Department at the University of Minnesota.
- *Our response to this disaster* was completely contingency driven. When the bridge went down, we rushed to replace it rather than take time to rethink how the river crossing

could better suit the area and what the transportation elements in our urban fabric should be. The disaster-response communications and management systems installed by the City of Minneapolis worked extremely well and have become a national model for local governments. Political leaders cooperated across party lines, at least initially, to mobilize funding and public processes to address the emergency of the collapsed bridge. But it was back to political business as usual and partisan sniping within weeks of the collapse.

- *Bridges nationwide* were examined after the collapse, especially in response to the National Transportation Safety Board's preliminary finding that failure of a particular gusset plate was at least part of the cause of the disaster. Some states passed emergency bonding bills to raise funding to repair structurally deficient bridges. But broader questions about the systems that support life in the United States—water, sewer, electricity, computer and fiber optic networks—remain unanswered and, largely, unasked. Some of the hundreds of miles of storm and sanitary sewer pipes and tunnels in Minneapolis alone are over a century old. Are they adequate for the expanding city or a disaster waiting to happen? Will it take a tragedy comparable to the collapse of the I-35W bridge to make us aware of needs in our other infrastructure systems?

- *Public investment* was an underlying question that came to the surface in predictable ways. To some extent the controversies about the cost of the bridge reflect deep divisions in our society between people who understand that public goods cost public money and people who see "the public" as nothing more than an agglomeration of private interests. The "that's my money they're spending on that bridge" argument continues to have currency and, as articulated in the press, simply became a reflection of the writer's disposition rather than an examination of the nature and costs associated with "the common good." On occasion isolated voices called for a reevaluation of the notion of the common good in light of the bridge disaster. David Morris posted a thoughtful reflection on the Web site OnTheCommons (http://www. onthecommons.org) in September 2007, and Minneapolis Mayor R. T. Rybak made the subject the theme of a talk he gave in a University of Minnesota lecture series that fall.

• *Whether we should spend or invest* in cases such as the bridge replacement was argued very pointedly by John Adams, professor of geography and public policy, in another of the university's lecture series. Adams pointed out that many of the specific physical features most often mentioned as components of the Twin Cities' livability—the parks and parkways, the well-planned networks of streets and commercial nodes that anchor the neighborhoods, and the system of public schools, colleges, and universities—are in place because of public investments made over the past fifty to one hundred years by community leaders who clearly understood that they were investing in the public realm on behalf of the public good, both now and in the future. Adams asked his audience to consider what our grandchildren and their grandchildren will have to say about the investments, or lack thereof, that we have made over the past twenty to thirty years.

• *Designing the bridge to also serve as a memorial* was part of the discussion from the beginning of the bridge design process. As the bridge construction progressed, and the political divisions about blame, accountability, and other factors grew sharper, the question of the most appropriate way to memorialize the loss of lives and the pain and suffering of survivors retreated into the background. To an extent, this is appropriate, as memorials such as these are often not served by being hashed out in public relatively soon after a tragedy. As the anniversary of the collapse approached in August 2008, some preliminary designs and a location for the memorial were released in relatively subdued public ceremonies.

But enthusiasm for the design was muted, funding to construct the project was not readily apparent, and the question of how to memorialize the tragedy threatened to fade from public view altogether. If this happens, reflecting a public desire to just move on, that will be a shame, because the collapse and reconstruction of the I-35W bridge is an important event in the history and development of the city and region and should not be left as an afterthought.

In sum, we're pretty good at engineering and can develop extraordinary measures to meet extraordinary demands and circumstances. But the bigger questions, about what are the best uses of public goods, who decides, who will pay for what, and how that process will be worked out, remain muddled. Some have argued that muddling through is the best we can do, given our complex legal, governance, and market-based systems. Coming changes in climate, demographics, and other global issues will tell us if this approach is sufficient.

NOTES

1. Nick Coleman, "A Penny-Wise, Pound-Foolish Government," *Minneapolis Star Tribune*, October 11, 2007.

2. On this topic and many of the other specific details in this essay, see "I-35W St. Anthony Falls Bridge," http://projects.dot.state.mn.us/35wbridge/index.html.

3. For more detail, see "Interstate 35W Bridge in Minneapolis," http://www.dot.state .mn.us/i35wbridge.

4. See, among many examples, Joe Soucheray, "$57 Million Extra for a New Bridge? Well, It'll Look Nice," September 23, 2007, http://nl.newsbank.com/nl-search/we/Archives?p _action=list&p_topdoc=21.

5. See "Interstate 35W Bridge in Minneapolis," http://www.dot.state.mn.us/i35wbridge.

The City: Neighborhoods and Transportation

CHAPTER FOUR

Neighborhoods Confront a Disaster Aftermath

Judith A. Martin

August 1, 2007, was a typically warm summer day in the Minneapolis riverfront neighborhoods close to the University of Minnesota's Twin Cities campus. K–12 schools were on summer break. The university's summer session was winding down, and the crush of returning students was still a couple of weeks in the future. Many neighbors were "up at the lake"—this is the time of year when Upper Midwest residents store up memories of warmth to get through the long winters. Local businesses welcomed their customers. Traffic flowed easily, as it does in the summer when many are away. Nothing could have prepared these neighborhoods, or their residents, for the change that was about to happen in their small world as the I-35W bridge unexpectedly collapsed just after 6:00 P.M. that evening.

Whenever tragedies occur, ordinary neighborhoods across the country suddenly land on the front page or become the lead on the television news. Places normally far distant from the media spotlight are swiftly inundated with emergency services, press, and crowds of curious onlookers. Normal life changes abruptly, often for quite some time. Exactly this dynamic began to play out in Minneapolis's Marcy-Holmes and Cedar-Riverside neighborhoods on that evening. This

FIGURE 4.1 » I-35W collapse and nearby bridges; Southeast Minneapolis at lower right, August 17, 2007. Courtesy of the Minnesota Department of Transportation.

chapter explores varied impacts of the bridge collapse, positing that fairly invisible and unmeasurable longer-term impacts dwarfed the attention-getting short-term impacts of such tragedies.

A Personal Note

I must start this discussion with full disclosure: I have lived just over one mile from the I-35W bridge for more than two decades, and I have driven over the I-35W freeway or under the bridge several times daily for all of that time. On rare occasions I also drive on the bridge itself. Nicollet Island/Marcy-Holmes is my home neighborhood, and my work life is rooted across the river in the Cedar-Riverside neighborhood. So, like many Twin Citians with lives partly defined by proximity to the Mississippi River, I do quick dashes across a bridge routinely and often. Along with most of my neighbors, my life and activities continued to be affected by the bridge collapse long after the event itself. We all had to stop and think about trips we intended to make, and we all had to accommodate more and larger vehicles in our daily travel. Our disruptions were not catastrophic, but they were nevertheless deeply felt and experienced. Everyone who lives or works in these neighborhoods—and the university alone employs over twenty thousand—became an unwilling participant in a very long experiment in tolerance.

Macro Effects

Neighborhoods affected by the bridge collapse regularly experience traffic and congestion challenges whenever the nearby university hosts a major athletic event, but this is scarcely newsworthy. Everyone simply adjusts routes or practices patience. The rift in routine that accompanied the sudden bridge collapse was unprecedented, drawing the attention of the entire world to this small spot on the map for a short time. As the media noted ceaselessly, Twin Cities' residents behaved helpfully throughout the immediate disaster period. The tendency toward helpfulness did not dissipate completely when the cameras turned off and the reporters went home. But the reality of a missing bridge and then the construction of a new one created difficult conditions for the communities adjacent to the missing highway link.

Local habits of easy access suddenly evaporated as many thousands of commuters and numerous construction vehicles inundated these neighborhoods on a daily basis. Neither residents nor businesses could have prepared for the massively increased traffic congestion or access disruptions. And when the reality of the collapse and rebuilding set in, the year of coping that then ensued was not news. It was simply the new life as we knew it until the bridge was rebuilt and reopened and traffic returned to something approaching normal.

Impacts of the bridge collapse resonated near and far around the greater Twin Cities. New routes had to be found for the 150,000 daily vehicles that had used I-35W, not an easy assignment in an already congested regional traffic system. Crisis management went into high gear: shoulder lanes on I-94 and on Highway 280 were temporarily converted to travel lanes, rush-hour traffic-light timing was extended while some signs and signals were altered, and traffic patrols assisted with direction in particularly congested locations. Even streets that were merely local routes were affected. Two easy local neighborhood escape routes were closed, first for cleanup, then for construction: West River Parkway through Cedar-Riverside and Second Street Southeast underneath the bridge site. This caused problems for many who had used these lesser-known streets to avoid the usual traffic. To add insult to injury, even the bike-and-pedestrian-only Stone Arch Bridge and Bridge 9 (the Dinkytown Bicycle Connection) were closed for a time.

Some of the worst "hot spots" were in fact well away from the immediate disaster site. These included the intersection of Franklin Avenue East and East River Parkway (a half-mile from the university), and the East Hennepin Triangle between the river and Central Avenue across from downtown.[1] These spots became overcrowded due to the former's proximity to the university in a bridge-constrained world, and the latter has long been a northern route away from downtown. The toll that these adjustments took on residents, busi-

MAP 4.1 » Central Minneapolis bridges (Google Earth).

nesses, and yes, commuters, could not be easily measured, but it was nevertheless quite real. For a short time, almost no one could reliably know what streets were open or closed unless they actually saw—or didn't see—a detour sign.

Context

Minneapolis really is a river city, and not just in image. In the core of the city, there are five bridges in a two-mile stretch of the river (Map 4.1). Daily life here often necessitates crossing a river or two, usually more than once a day. Until August 2007, most Twin Cities residents did this so routinely as to be oblivious to the large distance between themselves in their cars or on their bikes and the river far below. Many drivers likely crossed the Mississippi River, on the I-35W bridge or other bridges, without actually being conscious that they were crossing a river of note. Crossing the Mississippi here is usually a quick trip. The river is fairly narrow just above and below the Falls of St. Anthony, and the gorge that begins below the falls is moderately steep, obscuring the river unless you are standing very close. Other local river crossings, notably those over the nearby Minnesota River and St. Croix River, are harder to ignore because these rivers have broad flood plains and the bridges have quite long approaches. Thus an intriguing consequence of this tragedy is that more people likely became much more aware of the Mississippi's location and its relationship to the city and its neighborhoods.

It may have been surprising to many watching the bridge collapse news unfold that the toll of victims was relatively low, especially given the rush-hour timing of the event. The ongoing MN/DOT bridge repair work was likely responsible for this piece of luck. For several months, this particular stretch of I-35W had been limited to one lane going north and south; many commuters had found alternative routes. It was perhaps also a bit surprising that when the collapse occurred, no one in the immediate neighborhood was among the victims, although some were among the helpers and among those endlessly interviewed for a week about what impact the loss of the bridge had on them. Again, MN/DOT gets the credit. Because access to the bridge—on Fourth Street heading south and on Washington Avenue heading north—had been completely shut off for several months preceding the collapse, locals on both sides of the river had long since chosen other routes.

It is also fair to assume that most local residents did not even normally use the I-35W bridge. With the four-lane Tenth Avenue bridge immediately adjacent, most locals use that bridge for quick river crossings rather than merging onto the freeway. So the loss of the I-35W bridge for the adjacent neighborhoods was already a reality, and only a modest inconvenience at that, until the collapse. But when the I-35W bridge disappeared as an option for everyone else, this small inconvenience became a major challenge for these neighborhoods and their residents. One local observer quickly assessed:

> Our neighborhood has become a large staging ground for emergency workers and countless media caravans. Our mobility within the area has become limited, as the Stone Arch Bridge is closed, Second Avenue SE is closed on either side of the freeway, and the 10th Avenue bridge is closed. This is a time when many Marcy-Holmes residents, including myself, are glad that we live in what feels like a little urban village; many of us work downtown, shop at Lunds (and Surdyk's), eat at restaurants on East Hennepin, send our kids to school at Marcy Open and even go to church at First Congregational Church. There's very little we need that we can't walk to. And it's good we have most everything we need close by because the challenges of getting out of our neighborhood are going to be huge in the next few years. Life is going to be very different without I-35W roaring through our community. There are so many everyday errands we're going to have to rethink, simple trips that always began by getting on the freeway.[2]

Some of the city's most accessible areas suddenly became difficult to access, or to exit, as decisions about coping were made. The sensible administrative decision to close down the adjacent Tenth Avenue bridge for a couple of weeks to ensure privacy for recovery efforts had unforeseen consequences. It fundamentally severed the basic connection between Southeast Minneapolis and Cedar-Riverside and severely limited movement in this area for pedestrians and bicyclists as well as car drivers. The easy access that most of us living in the very center of the city take for granted evaporated overnight. Normal neighborhood life even disappeared for a while because people simply could not get to local stores, and some local businesses soon closed due to lack of customers and parking. For what seemed like a very long time, areas of the city that were formerly very comfortable, and had been taken for granted as such, became overcrowded, congested, and not particularly attractive, even for those who knew them well.

When the four-lane Tenth Avenue bridge did reopen, it was restricted to one lane in each direction, which might have sufficed for local use. But in the new post-collapse world, this bridge became the de facto alternative freeway connection between the Fourth Street Southeast freeway entrance and exit and the Washington Avenue entrance and exit across the Mississippi River. Thousands of cars were suddenly competing for space on what are essentially local streets. This inconvenience cannot, of course, compare to the loss of life and major injuries sustained by those on the bridge when it fell. It is a reality, however, that for more than a year, many thousands more were affected by this event than the official count ever noted. Collateral damage seldom is. There is another irony in the new situation that was created: freeways intended, in part, to reduce congestion on city streets (and yes, to move cars more quickly through dense areas) were now failing to keep their end of the bargain, as local streets became mini-freeways.

A larger bit of context concerns how we all think about daily infrastructure use. Panic about infrastructure is *not* a normative American experience. Minnesota Senator Amy Klobuchar perhaps best captured this sensibility when she commented the day after the collapse, "A bridge in America just shouldn't fall down."[3] In light of the I-35W collapse, something near panic ensued. The stability of nearly every other u.s. bridge was questioned, then quickly assessed, with particular attention to those sharing the same design as the collapsed bridge. There is no doubt that this event has reshaped thinking about bridges and roads nationally.

A Closer Look at Immediate Neighborhood Challenges, Postcollapse

Impacts on local neighborhoods in the collapse aftermath can be categorized in multiple ways. Some were modest and some significant; they varied in length of time as well as intensity. The following captures some of the most challenging impacts.

THE "OTHER" BRIDGE PROBLEM

This core area of Minneapolis has some of the oldest bridge crossings in the entire Twin Cities metropolitan area, though many of the original bridges have long since been rebuilt to accommodate more, heavier, and different traffic patterns. The loss of the easily identifiable I-35W bridge placed many thousands of unwilling and uninformed commuters onto the four bridges closest to it: the Tenth Avenue bridge, the Third Avenue bridge, the Hennepin Avenue bridge, and the Washington Avenue bridge (see Map 4.1). Had there been no traffic at all on these bridges before the collapse, this new reality may have been manageable. But all of these alternative routes were already regularly in use. In fact, all but the Tenth Avenue bridge regularly experience morning and afternoon rush-hour challenges. Even a distant traffic expert noted the impact: "Since the collapse, he said he has noticed an increase in traffic congestion all over the city, even overflowing into the surrounding suburbs, as people try to get to work. 'It's chaotic,' Chiu said. 'The traveling public has to take different routes, but the other routes are already congested.'"[4]

Local residents quickly learned to time any necessary car trips to avoid the worst of the post-collapse crush, usually successfully because we had the advantage of intimate local knowledge. One personal example: because I could see the level of traffic congestion on the Tenth Avenue bridge from my campus parking lot, I could make an informed choice to go home by another route when the bridge was backed up three-fourths of the way across. Most commuters did not have that option once they'd turned the corner onto the bridge approach. I know that I surprised one reporter early on by noting that it was faster for me to travel home *through downtown* than to wait to cross the traffic-congested Tenth Avenue bridge! Not many would think to navigate the edges of a rush-hour downtown to save time, but for one year, this was often the quickest way.

Within a short time, many freeway commuters had scoped out alternative routes. Some even learned to use the slightly farther away (and formerly underused) Plymouth Avenue bridge to cross the Mississippi. But many others simply stuck with the altered version of the familiar, creating even more congestion in their wake. After a couple of weeks, the newly congested alternative bridges became the new normal. No doubt many of the streets leading to and from these few still-open bridges achieved "failed" levels of service for the year that the I-35W bridge was being rebuilt. These streets clearly now have the potholes to prove this. So, one lesson from the I-35W collapse is that people can learn new routes rather quickly, if they have some information and a bit of adventure, but most stick with what they know.

CONGESTION AND FREEWAY BEHAVIOR ON LOCAL STREETS

The loss of the I-35W bridge tested the civility of this community in ways that were not attractive, beyond the initial rescue period. The I-35W freeway was interrupted in this central section of Minneapolis, but freeway traffic certainly did not disappear. People still had to get to work downtown and to get home. So freeway-destined traffic quickly appeared on local streets, many of which have designated bike lanes and hundreds of pedestrians throughout the day. Based on a year of close observation, it became abundantly clear that freeway drivers do not recognize people on foot or on bikes. These drivers simply do not expect to see alternative modes of personal transportation on a daily freeway commute, and they seemed to throw the rules of the road to the winds in their frustration with new circumstances. The new traffic on local streets was composed of unwilling folks just trying to get to work or to get home, and their behavior often reflected this reality.

It is some sort of a miracle that more pedestrian and bicycle accidents did not happen during this year, which can only be credited to the locals learning to walk and bike even more defensively. One could and did witness something close to road rage throughout this year, as freeway-bound commuters—who had to exit on the east bank of the Mississippi, cross the Tenth Avenue bridge, and get back on I-35W across the river, and then do the reverse on their return trip—stewed at having to wait for slow-moving students before they could make their required turns. It was mind-boggling to witness cars lining up to "merge" on a regular city street. Some freeway drivers tried to adjust. But there were also those who simply started a turn from the center lane and then had to stop quickly for the pedestrians they could not see and were not expecting.

What can be learned from this unexpected collision of travel modes? As a society, we tend to think very differently about people, cars, and people in cars. Urbanists, planners, and city lovers are almost always in favor of more people, with the friendly jostling for space that can occur when sidewalks are crowded. The assumption, derived from what we've all learned from Jane Jacobs's classic *The Death and Life of Great American Cities*, is that more people activate urban space, making it safer, more lively, and good for local businesses.[5] These same folks typically have far less positive responses toward large numbers of cars with drivers, even while they may admit that drivers are also people. Highways and freeways have long been viewed as anti-urban forces, draining away the life, work, and commerce of urban centers. These seemingly immovable positions (city lovers hating freeways, freeway lovers hating congestion) share nothing.

For a time in Minneapolis, car drivers had to get off the freeway and go slower. Had they not been in full commute mode, thinking mainly of intended destinations and their slow pace, might some commuters have developed curiosity, perhaps even wondered about the neighborhoods they were now traversing close up? It is possible to imagine suburbanites discovering new restaurants or even thinking that some of the neighborhoods they were now seeing more closely might offer a respite from lengthy commutes. It's unlikely that much of this happened.

It did become very clear during this year of observing travel behavior that mixing modes is a dicey business for those whose habits are already formed, including cyclists and pedestrians. This is especially true when a mixed reality is thrust on people without notice. Mixed-use and often mixed-travel modes became a staple of planning theory and practice in recent decades. In a carefully planned environment these can indeed work. But these workable results would be situations where people have the time they need to settle in and develop new habits. A hasty and unplanned interaction of mode choices seems something to be avoided, especially when the mix includes eighteen-wheel container trucks too heavy for the roads they are being forced onto.

THE "YOU CAN'T GET THERE" PROBLEM

For most of one year, beginning in late October 2007, after the remnants of the former bridge structure were removed from the site and the cleanup completed, local neighborhoods effectively and necessarily became a construction zone. Neighbors, whether traveling in the area or staying home, had to develop extreme patience. The company rebuilding the bridge, Flatiron Construction, had massive financial incentives to complete the job before the December 2008 deadline, so work went on twenty-four hours a day, seven days a week, starting October 30, 2007. The company was a model of communications expertise, sending weekly updates about progress to anyone signed up for e-mail alerts and posting notices online and in local papers about eruptions of especially loud noises.

But reconstruction was a given, and with it came noise and frequent closures of local streets that were needed for the rebuilding process. For the local neighborhoods, losing both Second Street Southeast and West River Parkway for a year was a daunting situation. These streets were and are local escape routes for everyone living nearby to avoid traffic jams on a normal basis. As a national engineering publication noted, "Streets near the bridge are closed occasionally for trucks hauling materials and pre-cast segments, conducting utility relocation, widening I-35w northbound and reconstructing curb cuts at various street corners."[6]

There are no real lessons here. Major construction and reconstruction projects occur all of the time all across the country. Typically there is knowledge about the project long in advance, and people have time to adjust expectations about movement and access. When something has to be done under a rapid timetable, the usual coping strategies are not available, and improvisation erupts. In this particular case, it worked better than might have been expected under the circumstances, but planned, staged construction is clearly preferable.

Beyond the Immediate Neighborhoods

All manner of businesses were affected by the collapse and its aftermath, even some located some distance away. Throughout the year of bridge reconstruction, local businesses in the immediate neighborhoods of Cedar-Riverside, Southeast Minneapolis, and Stadium Village were seriously harmed by the added congestion. These are the sorts of local businesses (restaurants, cleaners, day care, etc.) that thrive on pedestrian travel and typically have on-street parking nearby.

The new levels of greatly increased local traffic removed a large amount of on-street parking and scared away many pedestrians. Some closed altogether: a dry cleaner on Fourth Street next to the aforementioned freeway exit went out of business; the nearby day care center was taken for equipment storage and ultimately became a wetland to handle freeway runoff. Others survived by their wits and by incessant reminders in the neighborhood newspapers that places were open even while hidden by traffic. But the negative impact of congestion was quite widespread. The following excerpt captures the challenge that businesses even some distance from the bridge faced:

Any afternoon rush hour, Gwen Engelbert can look out the front window and see traffic cops wildly waving drivers past her E. Hennepin Avenue boutique. The patrols are needed to help manage a surge of traffic congestion in the East Bank and Marcy Holmes neighborhoods in Minneapolis since the Interstate 35W bridge collapsed Aug. 1. But it doesn't exactly help a business trying to catch a few drivers' eyes with window displays and sale banners. "We went from slow growth to a downward turn," said Engelbert, who co-owns Key North, at 514 E. Hennepin Ave., with her partner Katie Greene. Unlike businesses . . . who are hurting from fewer people driving past, shops in these neighborhoods are dealing with too much traffic on their doorsteps. The shop is among the dozens of Northeast businesses that have been affected by the bridge collapse.[7]

One response to this lingering business challenge, more than three months after the bridge collapse, was for the Minneapolis mayor to spotlight the problem and implore local residents to support local businesses even more. Whether this was effective is not known (within a year Key North moved one block away, near a popular restaurant). Fortunately, the rebuilding was quick. Businesses only had to make it through one year of chaos, and normality would resume sooner than typically happens in most long-planned and long-lasting construction projects.

Another sample of challenges presented by this rapid shift in circumstances concerns a local entertainment organization unexpectedly affected by the bridge collapse. The Minnesota Fringe Festival, the country's largest unjuried theater festival, was scheduled to start its eleven-day run on August 2, 2007, with several theaters in Cedar-Riverside and Northeast, among other places. The schedule was planned long in advance, knowing that people could get quickly from one venue to another across the river in the designated thirty minutes between shows. When this turned out to be impossible, artists and shows suffered a 30 percent decline in attendance. What lessons were learned in this arena? That collateral damage is inescapable and can be trusted to spread beyond the obvious and immediate candidates. FEMA disaster funds were made available to address the challenges of local businesses. Area businesses were asked to submit an estimate of lost revenues and economic injury by September 13, 2007.[8] But the process defined impacts far too narrowly to help many small businesses hurt by either too little traffic or too much. It is not possible to know how many businesses, near and far, were ultimately and negatively affected by this disaster.

Ultimately, the klieg lights went out and reporters moved on to the next story, while people near and far were left to cope. This seems the way of the world. One cannot help but wonder, though, if it had to be this way.

Opportunities Lost and Found?

An apt take on the year that the neighborhoods around the I-35W collapse site experienced from 2007-8 might be this: most local residents enduring the bridge's disruption and construction were just grateful that the new bridge opened rather quickly and that added congestion moved elsewhere. But there might be other ways to think about what happened and what might have happened. Was this a year of opportunities missed?

Not for the National Park Service. If the river was sometimes invisible before the bridge fell, this is one of the major post-collapse changes. Mississippi National River and Recreation Area (MNRRA), the keeper of the national park that encompasses the Mississippi through this upper stretch of the river, has taken full advantage of the recently increased perceptions about rivers and bridges. One can no longer cross most local bridges without encountering signs denoting the river's presence below. And the new replacement I-35W bridge was designed with public art (lighted pillars) installed to mark the river's edge partway across each span. Clearly an agency fighting for greater mission visibility found unexpected opportunity with the bridge collapse.

There is no doubt that many commuters brought by chance through the Marcy-Holmes and Cedar-Riverside neighborhoods were there for the first time. Is there any possibility that some might have taken time to discover intriguing new destinations or to appreciate the local specialties and haunts that have existed just off their well-trod path all along? Not very likely, because typical commuters are in the business of racing to and from preset destinations as quickly as humanly possible.

People traveling through are the precise opposite of people who might set out to explore a new part of the city as an adventure or to have a new experience. The former are not bad people. They simply have other priorities, like getting home, picking up kids, having dinner. Americans decades ago turned commuting into a habit, and habits are notably hard to undo. Car drivers racing through Marcy-Holmes had no hint that enchanting historic houses, indeed an entire historic district, sat just one block away. Might they have wanted to know this? People populating the lanes of unending traffic at Seven Corners (the intersection of Cedar and Washington avenues) may not have even realized the Southern Theater was right there, or that the Cedar Cultural Center was just blocks away—both venues for local and national music and dance.

Perhaps the city lost an opportunity in this unhappy situation to market the assets and unique qualities of these neighborhoods. Marketers are always trying to find new ways to capture eyes and attention; how better than to use a forced slow drive to remind folks what was right there all along? Now that everyone on the freeway is whizzing through these neighborhoods again, could anything induce those drivers to return for a slower look at where they'd been? The lesson here is that change is hard, and trying to change commuter habits may be even harder. Planners regard it as a great win to achieve a mode switch (car to bus or light rail). Thinking that exposure to new places might engender commuter curiosity is likely more than even the most optimistic urbanists could expect.

The I-35W bridge collapse and rebuilding experience is a stark reminder that too often we all stay in our travel ruts. We do not normally consider unfamiliar parts of the city ours to explore. The lenses that we bring to our thinking about cities are formed by our own personal experiences. But this particular experience of disruption for these close-in neighborhoods and for freeway commuters did not overlap in any productive manner. This demonstrates a clear loss of potential for larger urban life, if we understand urban life as creating connections that may not have existed previously.

_____

NOTES

1.   Jeremy Stratton, "Local Businesses and Officials Discuss Economic, Transportation Impacts of Bridge Collapse," *The Bridge*, August 14, 2007. *The Bridge* is a neighborhood newspaper that serves residents of the Marcy-Holmes, Prospect Park, and Southeast Como neighborhoods of Minneapolis.

2.   Linda Lincoln, "When Tragedy Happens in Your Neighborhood," *The Bridge*, August 2, 2007.

3.   CBS, ABC, and NBC evening news, August 2, 2007.

4.   Cody Calamaio, "UA Professor Helps Re-Route Traffic after Bridge Collapse," http://www.DailyWildcat.com, August 28, 2007.

5.   Jane Jacobs, *The Death and Life of Great American Cities* (New York: Vintage, 1961).

6.   Ivy Chang, "Victims Deal with Emotional Health and Their Compensation," *Week 36 Associated Construction Publications*, April 21, 2008.

7.   Dan Haugen, "Shop Local? Small Businesses Struggle with Traffic Near I-35W Bridge Collapse," *Minnesota Monitor*, November 20, 2007.

8.   Jeremy Stratton and Linda Lincoln, "City, Federal Assistance Possible for Businesses Impacted by I-35W Bridge Collapse," *The Bridge*, September 10, 2007.

CHAPTER FIVE

From Here to There to Nowhere: Competing Philosophies of Planning
Roger Miller

The metropolitan structure that we have created in the United States over the past forty-five years has been predicated on a set of well-known development processes. Huge federal subsidies for highway expansion opened up ever-widening areas for home construction at increasing distances from core cities, promoting edge city commercial concentrations that collectively dwarf the downtowns they once complemented and depended on. Homebuyers were willing to trade off higher transportation costs to the CBD (central business district) for lower house prices, more green space, and especially the ability to avoid spiraling inner-city problems and the need to pay to ameliorate them. In the new suburban landscape, modernist planning principles dictated that different urban functions each have their own separate location. It became an axiom that mixed uses automatically led to declining property values, particularly for the all-important residential homeowner, viewed as the cornerstone of the suburban tax base. The resulting built environment was characterized by a clear separation of land uses, with easy and inexpensive automobile transportation among them.

Today, a decade into the twenty-first century, the metropolitan landscape we have created is showing signs of stress. Bedrock assumptions, including inevitably rising house prices, perpetual availability of cheap gas, and the unquestioned superiority of suburban over urban environments no longer hold. In this chapter I will examine the roots of some of the problems that have opened up a new debate on metropolitan infrastructure and investment. I hope to show that, rather than being caused by the sudden downturn in the economy, wild swings in gasoline prices, or even by the I-35W bridge collapse, the cracks in the metropolitan structure reflect choices made as long as a century ago. By looking first at alternative planning paradigms early in the twentieth century and then at the model that became dominant around the time of the Second World War, we will be better prepared to evaluate some of the underlying assumptions and directions that face planners and citizens today.

The Metropolitan System Today

The fragility of the intricately networked Twin Cities metropolitan development solution has become painfully apparent—and not just through the temporary loss of one of the keystone elements of its high-volume transportation system. A year of living without the I-35W bridge across the Mississippi River highlighted some of the shortcomings of the dominant paradigm even before the triple shock of the rapid downturn in the real estate market, the sudden volatility in energy prices, and the resulting deep recession. Shortly after the bridge collapse, as drivers identified alternate routes, it became apparent that who was affected and how depended very much on location. Most people living in the core of Minneapolis generally managed quite well. While it is true that they had to deal with greater congestion in getting across the river, particularly during rush hour, relatively few people living within several miles of the I-35W bridge actually use it as part of their daily activity patterns. The freeway works best for those coming into the downtown from suburbs farther away, or traveling across downtown from the north or the south. But even with the bridge once again available for commuting, there is still a remarkable amount of congestion once traffic enters the grid of downtown streets. Our system of high-capacity, high-flow freeways is not particularly efficient at distributing traffic once it reaches the downtown area.

The Minneapolis–St. Paul metropolitan region is not particularly unique in how it has developed. How did we come to have such a dispersed metropolitan pattern of residences, commercial activities, and industry with high-volume roadways linking them all together? This is the pattern that we now take for granted in nearly all u.s. metropolitan areas. Were there other paths that development could have taken? Are there any solutions, or at least lessons to be learned, from looking back at how we got to the point we're now at?

Choices made over one hundred years ago have shaped the form of our cities and the kinds of public and private investments we have made. We have consistently chosen directions for growth that favor private property, individual wealth accumulation, larger-scale corporate solutions, and economies of scale over those that provide greater overall social efficiency or public investment for community gain. Unlike societies in which the state has played a much more central role in residential development, leading to concentrated areas of higher-density housing linked by public mass transit systems, as is the case in many European cities or in more recent Asian growth centers such as Seoul, Hong Kong, and Singapore, we have opted for a much more dispersed pattern of privately financed, individually owned single-family homes linked by a network of freeways and arterial roads catering to private automobile use. Many would argue that we have had a very good ride for the past fifty years in this automobile-driven development landscape. The middle class came to dominate American life, household wealth increased along with house values, and the level of material comfort enjoyed by a majority of the population has clearly grown. The engine of growth for American cities changed from industrial production to real estate and housing development, along with associated financial services based on the new development machine. But there have been danger signs, indications that our choices were not sustainable, as we've allowed our cities to balloon outward in search of an expanding tax base and rising property values.

Public or Private, and the Question of Scale

Early in the twentieth century, debates centered on whether private corporations or municipalities should develop urban infrastructure. In the United States the debate was largely settled in favor of private corporations—in large measure because municipalities, with their limited taxing and revenue-generating capacity, had a difficult time financing such improvements on their own. Also, the economic ideology of the time favored private investment strategies—even when they resulted in monopolistic practices. Thus, public works from streetcars to the first water systems were initially developed by private investors. Only in a relatively small number of sectors did municipal ownership and operation become the norm, usually including water, sewer, and other utilities deemed unprofitable or of such public benefit that municipal development (and public accountability) was preferable.

In some spheres there was considerable controversy and debate over the appropriate models for development. Thomas Edison, for instance, championed direct-current power plants for his proprietary electrical generating system, but was ultimately beaten out by Nicola Tesla's alternating current model that allowed power to be transmitted over hundreds of miles with negligible losses—facilitating large-scale, monopolistic corporate development and the growth of General Electric. In terms of urban transportation systems, a dispersed system was promoted by highly monopolistic, large-scale automobile producers. General Motors, Ford, and other companies systematically gutted rail-based mass transportation systems in order to sell buses and automobiles.[1] Key to their success, of course, was the decision on the part of state and federal governments to invest in the infrastructure that would allow these solutions to work—the highway systems created in every metropolitan area of the country.

Regional Planning, Garden Cities, and a Dispersed Model of Growth

Models of urban development patterns have changed over time, depending on levels of technology, economic conditions, and especially national policies associated with home ownership. Early in the twentieth century Patrick Geddes advocated a regional development pattern based on the interrelated economic functions found in what he considered the basic physiographic unit—the river valley. Basing his ideas on the writings of pioneering nineteenth-century French geographers—Élisée Reclus and Paul Vidal de la Blache—Geddes noted the appropriate locations of different economic functions in his Valley Section model. From mining and forestry located in upland sections of the valley, to agriculture, industry, and port facilities located closer to the mouth of the river, this model made sense in terms of the technological level of nineteenth-century society.[2]

Ebenezer Howard, writing at the end of the nineteenth century and basing his model of urban and regional development on his observations of London, growing like a cancer across the landscape of

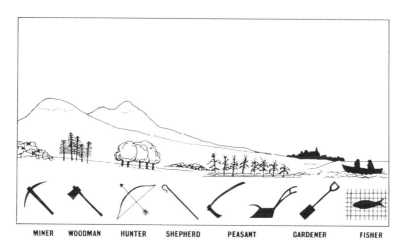

MINER   WOODMAN   HUNTER   SHEPHERD   PEASANT   GARDENER   FISHER

FIGURE 5.1 » "The Valley Section" with basic occupations. From Patrick Geddes, "Civics: As Applied Sociology," *Sociological Papers* (1905): 101–44. Reprinted in Peter Hall, *Cities of Tomorrow: An Intellectual History of Urban Planning and Design in the Twentieth Century*, 3rd ed. (Oxford: Blackwell Publishing, 2002), 149. Courtesy of the Sir Patrick Geddes Memorial Trust, Scotland.

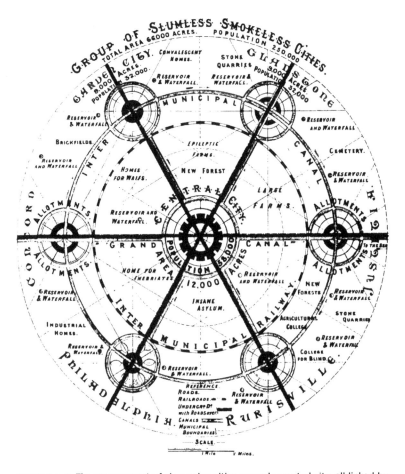

FIGURE 5.2 » The arrangement of six garden cities around a central city, all linked by rail. From Ebenezer Howard, *Garden Cities of To-Morrow* (London, 1902). Reprinted in Robert Fishman, *Urban Utopias in the Twentieth Century: Ebenezer Howard, Frank Lloyd Wright, Le Corbusier* (New York: Basic Books, 1977).

southeastern England, argued for limiting the size of satellite cities, surrounding them with permanent green space, and linking them to the central metropolis by high-capacity rail.[3] His Garden City model was unique in another feature—the idea that the increase in property values that followed development should be captured by the municipality rather than by individual householders. It was this last fact that probably kept his otherwise very attractive model from being implemented in anything but a few provisional trial examples; one

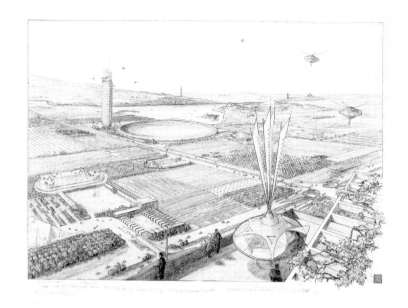

FIGURE 5.3 » Frank Lloyd Wright, "Broadacre City," 1935. Copyright 2010 Frank Lloyd Wright Foundation, Scottsdale, AZ/Artists Rights Society (ARS), NY. Photograph copyright Frank Lloyd Wright Foundation, AZ/Art Resource, NY.

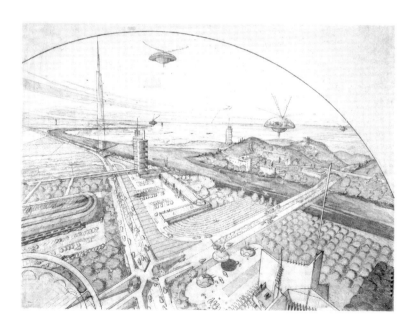

of the primary goals of homeowners was not just providing attractive shelter to their families, but generating long-term household wealth through real property ownership.

In the twentieth century, two further models have been especially influential. One is Frank Lloyd Wright's Broadacre City model, developed in the 1930s.⁴ Wright proposed giving each household an acre of land on which they would build a house (in the Prairie Style, of course) and raise most of their own food. The resulting low-density housing pattern required that each household own an automobile for traveling efficiently to the county center, where businesses and cultural institutions would be located. (In some of his iterations of this proposal Wright indicated that households might travel about using small personal helicopters.) This "Usonian" society would be low density and almost Jeffersonian in its outlines. Advances in agricultural technology would mean that the farmer-residents of Broadacre City would have ample time to pursue higher cultural and intellectual activities by journeying to the county center.

What is remarkable about Wright's radical vision is that it has, in many ways, become the template for today's upper-middle-class suburbs and exurbs. Granted, suburban homeowners don't produce their own food—but that part of the Broadacre City plan can probably be attributed to its Depression-era concern with subsistence and self-sufficiency at a time when the economy was in collapse. Nor do all suburban homeowners have a full acre of land at their disposal—the average today is typically a third of an acre. The resulting increased density has meant more households living in suburbs than Wright proposed, and even more important, given that he did not foresee the proliferation in the number of cars per household, at least a ten-fold increase in the amount of traffic generated in the residential areas of Broadacre City. The other part of Wright's vision that seems not to have come to pass has to do with the intellectual and cultural pursuits in which residents would participate. Suburbia is not generally known as the locus of all that is best in our country's intellectual and cultural life. Perhaps the reason for this is that the suburbs became a landscape of consumption rather than of production, in contradistinction to what Wright proposed. Thus, instead of a civic center that would be the site of local cultural, political, and intellectual life, the suburban shopping mall became the quintessential focus of social interactions. This is an idea to which we will return.

Concentrating Population: Models Based on Increasing Density

Almost diametrically opposed to Frank Lloyd Wright's Broadacre vision for a low-density, dispersed landscape of self-sufficient Usonian citizens is Le Corbusier's concentrated City of Towers proposal, articulated in *The Radiant City (La Ville Radieuse)* in 1935.[5] Le Corbusier, as Swiss-born Charles-Édouard Jeanneret-Gris called himself, proposed a radical restructuring of cities to rationalize them and to paradoxically create more open space by concentrating population and activities in high-density buildings. In high modernist projects such as the Voisin Plan for Paris (1924), Corbusier proposed clustering office functions in skyscraper towers surrounded by open space and

FIGURE 5.4 » Le Corbusier, "Paris: Voisin Plan," 1925. Copyright 2010 Artists Rights Society (ARS), New York/ADAGP, Paris/FLC. Photograph copyright Photographie Foundation Le Corbusier, L2(14)46, FLC/ARS, 2009.

connected by elevated highways to residential districts where the population would live in five- or six-story ribbon apartment buildings. With population concentrated in this fashion, it would be possible to reserve large tracts of open space between the buildings. Industry would be located in other areas. Land uses would be strictly segregated; to Le Corbusier, the messy mixing of different types of activities and land uses was distasteful, and in this his thinking was echoed by land-use planners who hit on exclusionary zoning practices to keep incompatible land uses separate from one another, thereby protecting property values. Le Corbusier's City of Towers (as it came to be called—in a version that didn't correspond as closely as it should have to his own vision) became the template for high modernist urban and regional development in places as disparate as Stockholm, Brasília, Singapore, and Dubai.

The Battle for the New York Region

During the 1920s, as New York City was becoming one of the most congested cities in the world, two opposing models for the city's future were proposed. One of them was a lineal descendent of the ideas of anarchist geographers and theorists such as Reclus, de la Blache, and Pyotr Kropotkin, filtered through the Scots planning theorist Patrick Geddes and popularized by Lewis Mumford, one of the most famous urbanists of the twentieth century. Just as Kropotkin and Geddes had argued for small-scale, dispersed settlement patterns keyed to a river valley's varied topography, Mumford proposed that in the twentieth century, with new transportation and communications technology, it was no longer necessary for cities to grow ever larger. A more civil and humane urban environment would be produced by keeping maximum city size at about two million inhabitants. Surrounding a denser urban core would be a series of dispersed, smaller settlements. Modern communications technology would allow people to carry out their work without the need to commute to the urban core. Dispersing population over a large area, while still maintaining reservations of green space, would bring about the best aspects of both Howard's Garden City arrangement and private ownership. Mumford, together with other progressive planners (Clarence Stein, Benton MacKaye, Alexander Bing, Catherine Bauer, and Henry Wright, among others) formed the Regional Planning Association of America (RPAA) in 1923. The organization lasted ten years and promoted not only decentralization of the population of New York City but also a series of regional plans centering on river valley authorities. Among the plans developed by members of the RPAA were the community building experiments of Radburn, New Jersey, and Sunnyside, New York, near the Appalachian Trail.

In contrast to the decentralizing push of the Regional Planning Association of America, another group with a startlingly similar name advocated a counter strategy. The Regional Plan Association of New York published a multivolume study of development issues associated with the city's growth. Under the general editorship of British planner Thomas Adams, the volumes, eventually published as *Regional Plan of New York and Its Environs*, provided a blueprint for practical, incremental improvements that could be made to the New York region's infrastructure, zoning laws, and development patterns to protect the capital investments businesses had made in the city's core commercial areas while minimizing the risk that firms would move out of New York City and into its surrounding hinterland.[6] With a proposal to increase the number of radial heavy rail commuter lines serving Manhattan, as well as plans for rational growth of suburban residential and business centers, it would be possible to keep New York City as the center of a vibrant regional economy that stretched across five thousand square miles of territory from Connecticut to Princeton, New Jersey, with a population projected to be almost 21 million people in 1965 (up from 9 million in 1929). Office functions could be concentrated in towering skyscrapers surrounded by open space—and although Corbusier is never referred to directly, he is clearly an éminence grise of the Regional Plan Association's vision.

Predictably, the idealistic members of the fledgling RPAA were appalled by Thomas's plan, with its strongly pro-business orientation. Mumford compared the plan to "a badly conceived pudding into which a great many ingredients, some sound, more dubious, have

FIGURE 5.5 » "The Proposed Chrystie-Forsyth Parkway." A. J. Frappier, delineator, 1931. From Committee on Regional Plan of New York and Its Environs, Thomas Adams, general director, *The Regional Plan of New York and Its Environs*, 2 vols. (New York, 1929–31), 399.

been poured and mixed."[7] Mumford would have been even more distressed had he foreseen the direction that the New York City region's development would take under the often less than genial guidance of Robert Moses, probably the most influential planner and developer of the twentieth century. Moses held as many as twelve state and city government jobs simultaneously, from parks commissioner to chairman of the Triborough Bridge Authority, to "construction coordinator" for the City of New York (which gave him sole authority to negotiate in Washington, D.C., for New York City projects). He strongly favored the automobile as a means of transportation over rail systems, and the massive highway projects he implemented changed the shape and direction of American cities.

Moses managed to fundamentally alter the way the City of New York functioned. Beginning with parkway systems that opened up vast tracts of Long Island to suburban development, he continued throughout his career building bridges and tunnels and widening roads to enable residents of the new suburbs to commute into Manhattan. To build these projects, however, he had to destroy huge swaths of the city. Tens of thousands of residents were displaced by

FIGURE 5.6 »
Robert Moses
with a model
of his proposed
Brooklyn-Battery
bridge (never
built), 1939.
*New York World-
Telegram and
the Sun.* Library
of Congress,
New York World-
Telegram and Sun
Collection.

FIGURE 5.7 » Richard Garrison, "Downtown Intersection." From the Futurama Exhibit at the 1939 New York World's Fair. Harry Ransom Humanities Research Center, The University of Texas at Austin.

FIGURE 5.8 » Richard Garrison, "Two 14-Lane Express Highways Cross in 1960," from the GM Futurama Exhibit, 1939. Harry Ransom Humanities Research Center, The University of Texas at Austin.

his largest endeavors, which included both massive public housing projects and freeways that cut through heavily populated neighborhoods. Robert Moses is famously quoted as saying, "Cities are for traffic." And in defense of the draconian removals that his projects occasioned (he called this "swinging the meat-axe"), he once noted, "If the ends don't justify the means, what does?"[8] In addition to the many parkways, bridges, beaches, parks, dams, public housing projects, and tunnels that gave him the sobriquet "the Master Builder," Moses also participated in the construction of two world's fairs in 1939 and 1964.

The 1939 New York World's Fair and the General Motors Futurama Exhibit

Meant to lift the spirits of the nation as the Depression continued and the situation in Europe deteriorated, the 1939 New York World's Fair was the largest international exhibition since the First World

War. Many of the planning ideas being debated in the New York region and elsewhere came together in the grand vision that was one of the most popular exhibits of the Fair, General Motors' Futurama exhibit, designed by Norman Bel Geddes. In large measure it was based on an amalgam of the ideas of Le Corbusier, Frank Lloyd Wright, Thomas Adams, and Lewis Mumford and introduced Americans to a vision of what the country could look like in a scant twenty years. Tall office towers were linked to sprawling suburbs by interconnected systems of superhighways, many of them automated. Millions of visitors to the Fair were captivated by this vision of an automobile-based future, one that seemed to promise both the elusive prosperity missing from Depression-era America and a level of individual freedom of mobility never before seen. Even with the intervening hiatus caused by World War II, the vision had been initiated by the 1950s.

Why was the General Motors dream for the future chosen over other alternatives? The vision proposed in the Futurama exhibit offered a series of clear advantages. Like Thomas Adams's proposals for New York, it protected existing investments in concentrated downtown cores. With a pent-up demand for housing dating back at least ten years, it promised to open up vast suburban areas for a new landscape of consumption by making them quickly accessible to the job-generating central business district. Houses not only had to be built, they also had to be furnished and cars had to be bought to facilitate commuting and shopping. The entire solution was geared to pull the economy out of its doldrums. The key to the system was the provision of high-capacity roadways that would make automobile use practical. The federal government became a critical player, providing guaranteed mortgage insurance to stabilize the housing finance industry, ultimately subsidizing up to 90 percent of the cost of the new limited-access roadways that linked city and suburbs. The new system also facilitated a new economic paradigm, one in which large-scale developments with massive infusions of federal money promoted concentration of wealth in the hands of a relatively small number of corporations—a radical change from earlier small-scale housing production and piecemeal road building.

The Postwar Suburban Landscape

There were clear social and economic advantages to the new model of development for the majority of middle-class Americans, including exceptional opportunities for more people to own homes, a resulting expansion in household wealth, rapid growth in the scope of consumer products needed to furnish the new homes being built, an exponential increase in the number of automobiles on the road, and the creation of a society that was driven by the engine of consumerism. But a number of drawbacks appeared as well. As families with the economic resources moved out of the central city and into new suburban housing developments, the tax base of the urban core declined. A bifurcated socioeconomic landscape began to develop, with the suburbs capturing stable or upwardly mobile white residents while the urban core increasingly was home to marginalized and economically dependent populations, including racial minorities. The socially and economically needy were concentrated in precisely that portion of the metropolitan landscape with a declining ability to pay for the services they required, while the suburbs, with their rising property tax revenues, could invest in schools, recreational opportunities, and other amenities demanded by their more affluent residents. All of this exacerbated both the push factors that led households to leave the central city and the pull factors that drew them to the new suburbs. As more population moved to peripheral locations, shopping and jobs followed them. Suburban shopping malls began to pop up like mushrooms after rain, and by the early 1960s downtown retail districts found themselves facing a declining portion of market share.

The Consequences of Too Much Success

The greater number of people living in suburban locations meant that there were far more automobiles on the roadways during the morning and evening commutes, requiring expansion of the new freeways to accommodate the increased traffic. Expanding freeway systems seemed to make sense. The costs were borne disproportionately by the federal government. Local costs were paid for by an increase in the value of the land made accessible in the edge cities that were growing up at the urban periphery. The link between place of residence and place of employment that had controlled the residential location decision before the Second World War was broken—suburban residents relied on the expanding freeway system to provide them with access to an ever-widening set of job and shopping opportunities located around the metropolitan area. More growth generated more congestion, and the model that had been put into place encouraged solutions that stressed economies of scale—great increases in the capacity of key freeway routes to channel traffic into central cities or past the CBD on interstate ring road highways.

As we found out with the I-35W bridge collapse, this process of channelization brought with it an important vulnerability. Removing any segment of the high-capacity, high-volume system of freeways and highways, particularly one located close to the downtown core and on a major radial route serving the CBD, had the potential to wreak havoc for suburban commuters. During 2008, as the I-35W bridge was being rebuilt on a massively accelerated schedule, speculation in the oil commodities market led to a sharp spike in gasoline prices. For the first time in decades, a debate on the wisdom of an ever-expanding metropolitan region reached the consciousness of the general public, no longer confined to small groups of environmental doomsayers, tree huggers, and back-to-the-earth proponents. It is not clear whether the uncertainty around gasoline prices contributed to the collapse of the subprime mortgage bubble or not; however, in many parts of the country, the first houses to be foreclosed on were those that had been built, sold, and resold in the farthest-out suburban and exurban areas. In any event, the viability of some of the farthest-out suburban developments in the Twin Cities metropolitan region, areas that have experienced significant house price erosion, foreclosures, and a near standstill in building activity, is in question.

Is this situation a temporary one, or is it likely to be a bellwether for fundamental changes in the ways in which people in the Twin Cities make choices about where to live, where to work, where to

shop, and how to negotiate the journeys that have become a necessary part of daily life? Is a continuation of the current system of
transportation and activity location the best or the only course
available? If we continue to think about solving the metropolitan
transportation problem solely in terms of providing more and higher-
capacity roadways, we may be missing some of the most important
questions about how we function as a modern urban society. To some
extent this may be a result of the different scales at which planners
(especially transportation planners) and individuals in households
think. Transportation planners think in macro terms—they focus on
the regional sets of linkages that make the high-volume, high-speed
highway system possible. Individuals, who view the situation from
their own perspectives, may be years ahead of planners in creating
new solutions to the costs and constraints they encounter in their
daily lives. Let's examine a few of the things that we may not be paying enough attention to and their implications for long-term transportation system use and development, as well as the ways that they
relate back to some of the earlier, alternative models of metropolitan
growth articulated before World War II.

The Decline of Public Space

Public space is under siege, and more and more public spaces are
being privatized. The shopping mall (or its downtown equivalent, the
upscale galleria-type development) is not truly public, as people trying to exercise what they thought were their free speech rights have
found. While parks are public spaces, they don't necessarily encourage the kinds of interactions that require people from different social
groupings to mingle and interact. In addition, as tax revenues fall,
funds for maintenance and policing of parks are being cut. In suburban areas, parks may not remain the safe amenities and attractions
they have been in the past. In addition, as daily life becomes more
atomistic, people may substitute personal activity for social interaction.

Frank Lloyd Wright thought that county centers would be places
where the dispersed citizens of Broadacre City would congregate for

cultural events, social interaction, and political life. The shopping mall subordinates all of these functions to the primary purpose of selling goods and services. Activities that might impede consumption are explicitly prohibited, from political speeches to taking pictures of individuals who are shopping. This limitation of the ability of individuals to freely assemble and exercise their rights of free speech is justified because shopping malls are private property rather than public spaces.

This raises the question of where people can go for culture or entertainment. Suburban venues may not exist in sufficient number or proximity for most residents to take advantage of them locally. This would seem to be one of the major changes that we could make, as a society, in order to reduce our dependence on transportation to the urban core in order to participate in such activities.

Privatization of Entertainment Recreation

Despite the presence of multiplexes in suburbs and downtown, more and more people are opting for personalized forms of entertainment. The home theater experience can be as technically satisfying as watching a movie at all but the best multiplex theaters and at considerably lower cost (once the capital investment in equipment has been amortized). Also, as entertainment consumers (especially young ones) demand ever more personalization of what they consume, the role of outlets that depend on the economies of scale offered by mass consumption are increasingly called into question. This affects not only movie theaters but also newspapers, radio, television, and other forms of "monopoly" distribution channels. Fewer people may be driving to the suburban multiplex for entertainment, paralleling the decline of downtown entertainment destinations three decades ago.

Food has become a form of entertainment as well as a source of nourishment. But a tightening of belts brought on by the current recession has changed the eating habits of many. In hard economic times, dining out becomes a luxury that many have cut from their household budget. This may have affected urban core and suburban restaurants in equal measure. Evidence thus far indicates that the lower end of the nonhome dining spectrum is doing much better than more expensive establishments. Cheaper fast-food restaurants also tend to be located more ubiquitously, and thus longer-distance trips into the center city or to major suburban centers may be lessening because of the economic downturn, replaced by short trips to the local McDonald's or Taco Bell.

Shopping in Person or Buying on the Internet?

It has become a widely accepted fact that in our consumer society shopping does not fulfill needs as much as it serves as a major form of recreation and entertainment. But consumption is also how we define ourselves to others, and having the correct ensemble of clothing, accessories, and logos undergirds the image of ourselves that we project (or think we do). In contrast to how we shopped in the past, when we physically encountered goods displayed in concentrated locations—the regional shopping mall, the boutique district of the city, and later the big-box outlet that offered more limited choices but better prices—price-conscious shoppers who still want a large range of goods from which to select are increasingly turning to the Internet to compare availability and pricing of goods. Bricks-and-mortar stores are where they go to physically see the goods, but the actual purchases may be made over the Internet, based on total price (including shipping, but usually not state or local sales taxes). The implications for transportation in the long run may be that people will spend less time traveling to physical retail locations and instead will spend time surfing the Internet for more-focused information on the goods they are interested in purchasing. This trend is still in its infancy, but it poses a threat to the bricks-and-mortar outlets in the long run.

The Fading Dream of Home Ownership

The rapid rise in housing prices that occurred during the past decade made buying a home less affordable to many, especially younger or lower-income households. One of the effects of this was to encourage building suburban homes farther out from the urban core, where land prices were cheaper and greenfield development practices kept costs down. The collapse of the subprime mortgage market has sent house prices spiraling downward. Ironically, the same collapse has also tightened credit to such a great extent that only the most credit-worthy buyers can take advantage of the decreased prices and lower interest rates that have resulted. Coupled with uncertainty about the cost of automobile fuel, this has prevented higher levels of home ownership in these peripheral suburban areas. In most regions, this is where foreclosures are most concentrated and where the prospects for housing recovery seem weakest. This may have a long-term effect of decreasing automobile transportation in these lower-density, more-spread-out sections of the metropolitan region. We have already seen a reduction in the amount of traffic on the major radial routes into downtown areas in large measure because of the startling numbers of people who have lost jobs in the economic recession.

The Attraction of Living Downtown

A corollary of the decline in the popularity or affordability of suburban areas is an increase in the attractiveness, across a number of age groups, of living downtown. The central cities are the major beneficiaries of this, with new loft and condo districts available for better-off homebuyers and renewed pressure on apartment housing for those without the wherewithal to purchase. The idea of what constitutes central city living is also expanding to include not only residential districts adjacent to the CBD but also gentrifying areas in some of the traditional working-class sections of the city (Northeast Minneapolis, for instance) and along emerging "green" transportation corridors.

One result of this, at least before the economic downturn, was that a small but growing number of people, those whose workplaces or other key destinations made it possible, were choosing residential locations on the basis of the availability of alternative transportation modes such as bicycle, LRT (light rail transit), even bus. Obvious examples are locations along the Hiawatha LRT line, but they also include some new bicycle-accessible developments on the Midtown Greenway bike and pedestrian trail. Bus feeder lines to the LRT are also expanding the area of impact. Even suburban developments in Bloomington and elsewhere along the Hiawatha LRT corridor are bringing European-style rail-dependent residential development to closer-in suburbs. Longer-distance bus commuting from suburbs to central city locations (especially in Minneapolis) has also increased with higher fuel prices, despite compensatory increases in transit fares. While still only a relatively small proportion of total residential choices, this trend could change the valuation of central city or transit-oriented locations versus dispersed suburban ones to the advantage of the former.

A major reason for the new popularity of downtown residential locations is a growing recognition of the desirability of multiuse, multifunction local neighborhoods. One of the most important changes affecting transportation use and the need for investments in high-capacity network elements is the emerging planning consensus that such neighborhoods are preferable to the modernist paradigm of the strict segregation of land uses, such as we saw in Le Corbusier's ideas. Variously labeled New Urbanism or transit-oriented development, these varied and integrated styles of neighborhoods emphasize pedestrian-friendly layouts, the proximity of frequently used functions to residential neighborhoods, and the availability of spaces for congregation and socializing as well as consumption. The emphasis is on community, rather than privatized space. The implications, of course, are a minimization of longer-distance travel and a reduction in the need for high-capacity infrastructure elements such as the I-35W bridge. In the transit oriented development version of this model, collective transportation systems, such as LRT or heavy rail systems, often substitute for new freeway lanes.

Reading the Future in the Past

As we examine these alternatives, some a matter of choice, others of constraint, we can see echoes of the proposals for metropolitan growth formulated in the first half of the twentieth century. The emphasis on providing public spaces to promote social interaction and a growing sense of community derive from a strain of planning thought that goes back to Reclus, de la Blache, Kropotkin, Geddes, and Mumford. Ideas about population deconcentration and local self-sufficiency were promoted by Howard and Wright. Yet it seems that the majority of planners remain enamored of the ideas of Le Corbusier, with a place for everything and everything in its place and nowhere else. But the underlying and often unstated rationale for those choices is being subjected to explicit scrutiny for the first time in a society-wide and systematic way. Do we always achieve the highest societal returns when we centralize production and achieve economies of scale? Isn't that also a recipe for congestion and, ultimately, *dis*economies of scale? When we exceed the capacity of the transportation infrastructure we have built to accommodate further pushes into the hinterland, don't the resulting traffic tie-ups reduce the overall efficiency of the system? And when key segments of a transportation system that channels most of its users onto a few high-capacity routes fail, as they ultimately will, is there sufficient redundancy to provide alternative paths for enough people to keep the system functioning?

What is perhaps most interesting about most of the options listed earlier is that they have more to do with personal lifestyle choices than they do with transportation planning. They involve individual decisions about how and where to spend time in recreation and entertainment, how to shop, and preferences for social versus isolated activities. Perhaps one way to improve the metropolitan region's transportation system is to pay greater attention to those aspects of contemporary life that seem to have the least to do with getting from one place to another. One hundred and twenty years ago, most people never journeyed more than twenty miles from where they were born. We have come to assume that nearly unlimited mobility is the norm, at least for those of us in the advanced industrial countries. Has this degree of mobility really contributed to a higher quality of life, and how should we think about the relationship between our material well-being and other aspects that contribute to our sense of security, fulfillment, and happiness?

Now that we know that planning solutions always respond to

conditions as they exist at the moment, we need to consider what has changed in the ways that we structure our daily lives and how well those changes are reflected in our built environment. Accessibility solutions based only on considering the capacity of our roadways or how far out we can extend our suburbs will miss the important lifestyle changes that are occurring in contemporary American life. A catastrophic failure such as the I-35W bridge collapse provides us with both a warning and an opportunity to revisit and rethink what we believe about the physical and social structure of the urban environment we have created.

NOTES

The author would like to thank Pat Nunnally for providing the impetus for this chapter by organizing the symposium in which a much shorter version was presented and Stefano Bloch, Jaime Kooser, Marie Minervini, and Tim Mennell for their critical and supportive comments.

1. Glenn Yago, *The Decline of Transit: Urban Transportation in German and U.S. Cities, 1900–1970* (Cambridge: Cambridge University Press, 1984).

2. Patrick Geddes, "Civics: As Applied Sociology," *Sociological Papers* (1905): 101–44. Reprinted in Peter Hall, *Cities of Tomorrow: An Intellectual History of Urban Planning and Design in the Twentieth Century*, 3rd ed. (Oxford: Blackwell Publishing, 2002), 149. See also Patrick Geddes, "The Influence of Geographical Conditions on Social Development," *Geographical Journal* 12, no. 6 (December 1898): 580–86.

3. Ebenezer Howard, *Garden Cities of To-Morrow* (London: Swan Sonnenschein and Co., 1902).

4. Frank Lloyd Wright, *Broadacre City: A New Community Plan* (New York, 1935).

5. Le Corbusier (Charles-Edouard Jeanneret-Gris), *The Radiant City: Elements of a Doctrine of Urbanism to Be Used as the Basis of Our Machine-Age Civilization* (London: Faber and Faber, 1967). Translation of *La Ville Radieuse* (Paris, 1933).

6. *Regional Plan of New York and Its Environs*, 2 vols. (New York, 1929–31).

7. Quoted in Peter Hall, *Cities of Tomorrow: An Intellectual History of Urban Planning and Design in the Twentieth Century*, 3rd ed. (Malden, Mass.: Blackwell Publishers, 2002), 167.

8. Robert Caro, *The Power Broker: Robert Moses and the Fall of New York* (New York: Vintage Books, 1974).

PART III

The River: After the Collapse

CHAPTER SIX

A Fickle Partner: Minneapolis and the Mississippi River

John O. Anfinson

In early October 1933, Clarence Jonk launched the *Betsy-Nell*, his awkward houseboat, into the Mississippi River in Minneapolis. She floated on eighty fifty-five-gallon oil drums and was propelled by two Model T engines. While planning the trip, he had walked through the oak savanna in what is now a northern St. Paul suburb with two women friends. "After we had eaten our fill of berries," he wrote, "we lay upon the warm grass of a hillside in the shade of a large oak tree. We got to roaming in our fancies, traveling to far-away places. . . . I took them with me on the great river where I knew I would soon be going. . . . Once on the river they could not wait for the next bend to unfold and reveal the charms and romantic history of some old town." Soon, he said, "They wanted to go Gypsy-wild with me, and with me sail the long adventure of the great river."¹ The twenty-seven-year-old Jonk hoped to escape the Great Depression and find inspiration for his poetry and prose, but he could not escape what the river had become.

Over the last 150 years the Great River's power has compelled people from around the country and world to travel all or some part of its 2,350-mile length. Many have written stories or published photos highlighting places that illustrate the "Long Adventure." Lake Itasca, St. Anthony Falls, the site of the battle of the Bad Axe, Mark Twain's boyhood home in Hannibal, the Eads Bridge, the Civil War battlefield at Vicksburg, the Old River Control Structure, and New Orleans' French Quarter are just a sample. Not all the places tell romantic stories. Many emphasize the tragedies of American history. Romantic, tragic, heroic, or simply entertaining, travel accounts keep the stories of these places alive. Will the I-35W bridge site become a story of the Long Adventure? Will those who pass under the new bridge write about its story or photograph it in five, fifty, or one hundred years?

Two stories of the Mississippi River in Minneapolis offer some perspective on how we might remember or forget the I-35W bridge site as a place and as a story. They also offer a context in which to consider how our relationship with the river has changed. In 1869 another collapse occurred less than a mile upstream from the present-day I-35W bridge site. Here the riverbed itself fell. This collapse threatened the economic engine that drove the city's economy. Only one person died, but the disaster dragged on for seven years. Until recently, few in the Twin Cities area knew of this story, and most still do not.

The second story spans almost forty years. Tens of thousands suffered and thousands died, but the story has been lost. From 1871 to 1910, Minneapolis drew water from the Mississippi River and pumped it untreated into homes and businesses. At the same time, the city dumped its raw sewage, garbage, and other refuse into the river. This conflicted relationship—depending on the river while abusing it—exemplifies a larger disconnect. Travel accounts like Jonk's often say something about the traveler's and America's relationship with the Mississippi River. America is proud of the Mississippi, touting it as the "Great River" and the "Mighty Mississippi." Yet America has treated the river as something quite the opposite. The I-35W bridge disaster and reconstruction show, in small ways, that a more harmonious relationship is developing.

Thousands of people walked out on James J. Hill's Stone Arch

Bridge after the I-35W bridge disaster. It was one of the best places to view the wreckage lying only one-half mile downstream. Completed in 1883, Hill's bridge once carried trainloads of wheat to the east bank flour mills at St. Anthony Falls. Now it serves pedestrians and bicyclists. In the days after the disaster, I joined other National Park Service rangers on that bridge. Our goal was to help orient people who came to view the site. After taking in the I-35W site, people began looking around at the falls, the two locks and dams, the ruins in Mill Ruins Park, and the glassy Mill City Museum inside the burned-out remains of the Washburn A Mill. For many it was their first time on the Stone Arch Bridge, and they could not make sense of the geography, some even asking which way the river flowed. They had questions about what things lying in the river were, what the water quality was like, and what the barges carried, although the collapse had closed the river to traffic.

The presence of the Lower St. Anthony Falls Lock and Dam, just above the twisted beams and concrete, the Tenth Avenue bridge about three hundred feet below the I-35W bridge, and the old Northern Pacific railroad bridge another five hundred feet downstream confused even more visitors. After flowing southeasterly from above the falls to the railroad bridge, the Mississippi hooks sharply south, so onlookers could not see the river extending into the background. During those early August days of 2007, they saw a stained-glass pattern of green behind the bridge trusses and bridge fragments.

Interstate 35W spans the gorge, a unique reach of the Mississippi River. The crossing lies less than one mile below St. Anthony Falls, the only major waterfall on the Mississippi. From the falls, the river descends into a gorge framed by tree-shrouded bluffs of Platteville limestone, Glenwood shale, and St. Peter sandstone rising fifty to over one hundred feet above the river. The gorge runs for eight and one-half miles, ending abruptly at the Mississippi's confluence with the Minnesota River. Here the Mississippi enters the wide valley sculpted by an ancient glacial river.

Nowhere along its entire 2,350-mile course does the Mississippi drop so steeply through such a narrow canyon as it does through the gorge. From just above St. Anthony Falls to the Minnesota River, the Mississippi plummets more than 110 feet. The bluff tops lie only one- to two-tenths of a mile apart. Before locks and dams flooded the gorge, a treacherous rapids boiled through this reach at high water, jumping and careening off huge limestone boulders left by the retreat of St. Anthony Falls. At low water, you could have waded or hopped across on the boulders, resting on one of more than a dozen islands. At the I-35W bridge, the Mississippi is pinched tighter than anywhere else in the Twin Cities and never gets as narrow again.

St. Anthony Falls was born just below downtown St. Paul about twelve thousand years ago, some fifteen river miles below where it now lies. Called the Glacial River Warren Waterfall, it measured over 2,700 feet across and stood 175 feet high. The meltwater from the colossal glacial Lake Agassiz, lying in northwestern Minnesota and southern Canada, thundered over the limestone riverbed. As the water curled back, it ate away the soft sandstone beneath. Soon, the unsupported limestone broke off, the falls receded upstream, and the process began again. By 1680, when Father Louis Hennepin became the first European to see the falls, it lay roughly 1,500 feet downstream from its present location and less than 2,000 feet upriver from the I-35W bridge site.

The River Falls In

The Mississippi River and St. Anthony Falls were everything to the early residents of Minneapolis. Lumber milling began in earnest at the falls in 1848, when Franklin Steele finished the first dam and sawmill. By the late 1850s, sawmills occupied platforms built just above the edge of the falls and out to Hennepin Island from the east and west banks. There was no more space for new mills at the falls, but not all of the river's power had been harnessed. To expand milling, the Minneapolis Mill Company built a canal along the west bank in 1857, feeding water to a row of mills along the west bank. By 1869 the falls powered eighteen lumber mills, and lumber milling had become the city's leading industry. Flour milling grew even faster. In 1859 the Cataract Mill became the first commercial flour mill on the west side.

Seven flour mills occupied the west side canal twelve years later, and four flour mills operated on the east side. Minneapolis seemed poised to become one of the nation's leading timber and flour milling centers. In 1869, however, the only major waterfall on the Mississippi and the reason for the city's rapid growth almost disappeared.[2]

The crisis began underneath the Mississippi River. For a short distance, the riverbed above the falls has the same layers of limestone, shale, and sandstone that caused the falls to migrate up the river from St. Paul. The sandstone is over 99.4 percent pure silica—the "Ivory Soap" of sandstone—so there is little to bind together the smooth, round grains of sand, which causes the sandstone to fall apart easily. You can carve your initials in it with a stick.[3]

For over a year, workers had been tunneling through the sandstone. They had begun by heading into the exposed sandstone at the base of Hennepin Island, below the falls. Hennepin Island both straddled and divided the cataract. The workers advanced upriver under the island and then under the river. By the morning of October 4, 1869, they had tunneled some two thousand feet and were just under Nicollet Island, where the island's owners planned to erect a mill. That day water started leaking and then pouring into the tunnel's upper end, driving the workers out. The water quickly ate away the sandstone walls. The six-foot-square tunnel grew into an elongated cavern ten to ninety feet wide and sixteen and a half feet deep. The next morning the limestone riverbed gave way. A large whirlpool formed, sucking in everything nearby and spitting it out through the tunnel.[4]

People in Minneapolis abandoned their work and rushed to the falls. Volunteers built a large raft and floated it over the whirlpool, which sucked it to the riverbed. The volunteers laid planks out to the raft and began piling on dirt, rocks, and brush, but water continued coursing through the Eastman Tunnel. Volunteers built more rafts. About noon, a new hole opened, between the raft plugs and the shore. Refusing to give up, the volunteers constructed still more rafts and sank them over the new break. By the afternoon, they inspected their work, thinking they had defeated the river. The river took exception. About 3:00 P.M., as people scrambled off, the river pulled the fee-ble structures down through the limestone riverbed and carried the debris out the tunnel. An even larger break occurred an hour and a half later.[5]

This was only the beginning of a calamity that threatened to undermine the entire riverbed at St. Anthony Falls and with it the milling industry. The lumber and flour millers and all the related businesses would soon learn that the falls was only one tick of the geologic clock from ending its twelve-thousand-year journey. This is a story about greed and geology and engineering and the power of nature. Greed led to the disaster. Geology—no pun intended—under-lay everything. Engineering played two roles: poor engineering caused the debacle, and good engineering saved the day. We can at times subdue nature, but we can never completely control it.

This story began in the late 1860s. William Eastman and his part-ners wanted to join the booming saw and flour milling industry, but other companies controlled all the mill sites. Eastman and his part-ners, however, owned Nicollet Island, just upstream of the falls. Under Eastern water law, they asserted, since they were upstream they had priority right to the river's water. To avoid a lawsuit, the other mill-ers agreed to let Eastman construct a mill on Nicollet Island and run a 2,500-foot-long tailrace, called the Eastman Tunnel, from below the falls to Nicollet Island. Water would flow into the mill, down a shaft to turn the mill wheel, and exit out the tailrace below Henne-pin Island.[6]

On September 7, 1868, workers started digging the tunnel, and by October 4, 1869, they were under the downstream end of Nicollet Island. On October 5, the riverbed collapsed. Over the next six years, the falls continued eroding. In the spring of 1870, flood waters poured into the tunnel, expanding the cavern below the limestone. At the downstream end of Hennepin Island, the water scoured a large cavity below the Summit Mill and a warehouse, and both crumbled into the chasm. On July 3, 1871, water flowing through the tunnel hit a plug of debris and then scoured a hole out the west side of Hennepin Island. The water hollowed out a new cavern sixteen feet wide by eight feet

FIGURE 6.1 » Summit Mill and warehouse collapsed into the Eastman Tunnel during the 1870 spring flood. Courtesy of Minnesota Historical Society.

deep under the limestone. Although the riverbed did not cave in, the new hole added to the increasing number of cavities below the river-bed. Workers built a cofferdam around the first breaks in the riverbed and pumped out the water. But on April 15, 1873, a flood swept through the cofferdam on the west side of Nicollet Island, opening a gap 150 feet wide, destroying large parts of the repair work, and drowning one man.[7]

Workers repaired the cofferdam, but water continued leaking into the tunnel. Trying to discover the source, the U.S. Army Corps of Engineers conducted a survey of the riverbed above the falls. The survey showed that the limestone riverbed ended less than one thousand feet above the cataract and immediately above the broken riverbed. Water was running under the limestone cap on the west side of Nicollet Island, excavating pathways through the sandstone and connecting to the Eastman Tunnel. Unless checked, the erosion would soon undermine the entire riverbed, the remaining limestone would collapse, and St. Anthony Falls would disappear.[8]

On April 14, 1874, the Corps convened a special board of engineers. After considering all the options, they recommended building a dam under the river, under the limestone, from one bank to the other. The Corps began building the cutoff wall on July 9, 1874. The Corps first sank a shaft six feet by fourteen feet wide on Hennepin Island, cutting down through the limestone and shale and down another forty-five feet into the sandstone. Then digging toward the east and the west banks, the engineers hollowed out a space four to six and a half feet wide and forty feet high below the limestone. They filled the space with layer after layer of concrete.[9]

But the river did not give up. On April 9, 1875, an ice dam above St. Anthony Falls broke, and the river suddenly rose and flowed over Hennepin Island and down the shaft. Luckily, no one was working on the cutoff wall. Six days later the upper cofferdam on the east side of Nicollet Island gave way. Water flooded the cavity created by the break of 1871, destroyed repair works in the Eastman Tunnel, and exited through a new hole out the west side of Hennepin Island and out the tunnel's mouth.[10]

Despite the flooding, quicksand, and the water continually leaking into the work area, the Corps completed the cutoff wall on November 24, 1876. The *Minneapolis Tribune* underscored the project's significance: "The final completion of the great sustaining wall … removes the only obstacle that has ever seriously threatened the onward progress of the city of Minneapolis, or retarded its realization of the Manifest Destiny which is to make it the great metropolis of the northwest."[11] Milling at the falls resumed its rapid growth, and from 1880 to 1930, Minneapolis led the nation in flour milling. Spurred by the milling, Minneapolis became Minnesota's largest city during the 1880s and one of the largest in the Midwest.[12]

River of Life and Death

Like other big cities, as Minneapolis grew and industrialized, its population size and density overwhelmed the city's ability to offer two basic needs: water supply and waste disposal. The two became linked in an insidious loop, and as the citizens of Minneapolis became intimately dependent on the Mississippi, their disgust with the river mounted. Most cities relied on private or neighborhood or community wells and springs for their early water supply, and many individuals captured rainwater in cisterns. But as the demands of population growth, firefighting, and industrial expansion exceeded the capacity of these sources, cities started drawing water from lakes and rivers and piping it directly into businesses and homes. Philadelphia established the first waterworks in 1802, and other major eastern cities followed shortly afterward. By 1860 the sixteen largest cities in America had waterworks.[13]

Minneapolis built its first waterworks in 1871, near the head of the west side mill canal.[14] Known as Pump Station No. 1, its water-powered Holly pumps could produce 2.5 million gallons per day. Historian Rufus J. Baldwin called it "a crude and imperfect affair," in his early 1890s account of the waterworks. Still, he said, "There was a great satisfaction when on a public trial, five streams of water were simultaneously thrown from hydrants upon and over the Nicollet house."[15] By 1884 Station No. 1 had five new pumps that could deliver 33 million gallons of river water per day. The next year, Minneapolis opened Station No. 2 on Hennepin Island, bringing 10 million gallons more into the city per day. After only thirteen years, the waterworks was sending 43 million gallons per day to the city's residents and businesses, all of it untreated.[16]

The city's satisfaction lessened as the water's purity became an issue. In 1882 city officials tested the water from a downtown fire hydrant. The water, their report said, "exhibited considerable quantities of animal and vegetable impurities . . . *including an unusually large proportion of parasitic worms.*"[17] The city received so many complaints about the water that it established Pump Station No. 3 at Shingle Creek, or Camden Park, four miles above the falls, in 1888.[18] The plant could generate 12 million gallons per day, supplying, Baldwin boasted, enough water for fire department, public fountains, and "street sprinkling."[19] The city continued pumping water from Stations 1 and 2.

Not everyone liked the water, Baldwin admitted. "Many people," he said, "have a prejudice against using the city water for drinking and culinary uses," and "a considerable business is done in supplying such with spring water brought in jugs and tanks from several natural springs in the northerly part of the city." Those who could afford it or refused to use the city's water gathered water from Inglewood, Glenwood, and Big Medicine springs or from the artesian wells sunk at Loring and Bryn Mawr parks.[20]

Baldwin, however, dismissed complaints about the water. "In point of fact," he insisted, "the river water is as free from deleterious qualities as any water commonly employed for culinary purposes." The water, he pointed out, had been examined at different times and seasons. "Its purity," he maintained, "is greater than that of water

FIGURE 6.2 » Minneapolis finished Pump Station No. 4 on the Mississippi River's east bank in Fridley, Minnesota, in 1904. It is the only one of the first four pumping stations still in existence, and it is still visible to those traveling on the water. Photograph by Charles J. Hibbard. Courtesy of Minnesota Historical Society.

taken from the neighboring lakes, and much freer than that of the springs from mineral solutions."[21] Baldwin was tragically wrong.

In 1897 the city completed its first step toward improving the river's water quality when it built two reservoir basins in Columbia Heights, a northeastern suburb of Minneapolis. Each reservoir held 47 million gallons, a total of 94 million gallons. The reservoirs served as settling basins only. They were not filtering basins, which could have removed some of the pollutants and bacteria. Minneapolis obtained water from the reservoirs via Pump Station No. 3 at Shingle Creek.[22]

In 1904 Minneapolis added Pump Station No. 4 on the east bank of the Mississippi River in Fridley, five river miles above St. Anthony Falls. The two Holly pumps delivered 15 million gallons of river water per day to and from the two reservoir basins. The city then shut down Stations 1 and 2 at the falls, eliminating the most polluted sources of water.[23]

As of 1904, Minneapolis had been drawing raw river water from the Mississippi for over thirty years and piping it into homes and businesses. While the pumping stations at Shingle Creek and Fridley improved the water quality, the quantity of pollution pouring into the Mississippi River from Minneapolis and the cities above had been increasing steadily. A 1909 report on water from the Fridley plant noted, "The colon bacillus is constantly found in every c. c. of water examined, indicating considerable fecal pollution."[24] A single individual could infect the entire water supply.

Like most cities, Minneapolis failed to consider where the great new volume of water provided by their pumping stations would go after being fed into homes and businesses. Prior to municipal water lines, people used an average of two to three gallons of water per day. They threw this wastewater out their doors, into their yards or the street gutters, or pipes carried it to a cesspool or privy vault where their human waste went. At two to three gallons per person, these methods of disposal sufficed. Piped-in water, however, increased personal consumption up to fifty to one hundred gallons per day. After getting running water, many people bought toilets and ran lines to their privy vaults or cesspools, which could not contain the volume of liquids now gushing into them. Cesspools, privy vaults, and streets began overflowing, and the ground became saturated, flooding into basements and wells. This was especially true in the more dense sections of cities with large businesses and multifamily dwellings.[25]

Some people connected their wastewater lines to city storm sewers, but in many cities, this was illegal. According to Joel Tarr, one of the leading environmental historians of wastewater issues, no cities had sanitary sewer systems before the 1850s, and most cities did not construct them until after 1880. As the problem became worse, the push for sanitary sewers forced cities to begin building them, but, Tarr says, all cities over thirty thousand people built combined storm and sanitary sewer systems. As a result, cities often emptied their waste water into their source of drinking water. Defending this practice, sanitary engineers argued that it was too expensive to construct separate systems, and they contended that streams and rivers could purify themselves anyway. In Boston, New York, Philadelphia, Chicago, Minneapolis, and elsewhere, this same scenario played out.[26]

Unlike many eastern cities, Minneapolis had not developed a storm sewer system when it began drawing water from the Mississippi River. So the city combined its storm and sanitary sewer systems at the outset. Between 1870 and 1895, Minneapolis constructed 124 miles of sewers that funneled the city's wastes directly into the Mississippi River.[27] The sewer system itself may have accelerated the switch to city water. In his history of the Minneapolis waterworks, Rufus Baldwin says, "When the sewers began to be constructed they drew off the water in the soil so that many wells went dry, and forced their owners to resort to city water."[28] Sewage leaking into private wells may have forced people onto the city system also.

CONSEQUENCES

Minneapolis and all other big cities quickly learned the consequences of drinking from the waters they polluted. Cholera, yellow fever, dysentery, and especially typhoid fever began breaking out among their populations. Lowell and Lawrence, Massachusetts, drew their water from the Merrimac River. Between 1890 and 1891, both suffered a severe typhoid epidemic. One hundred and thirty-two people died in Lowell and seventy-four in Lawrence. Pittsburgh took its water from the Allegheny and Monongahela rivers, and from 1894 to 1906, Pittsburgh experienced more than five thousand cases of typhoid fever each year.[29] On October 15, 1901, the *New York Times* reported that typhoid fever epidemics had broken out in many major cities, including Boston, Baltimore, Cincinnati, New Orleans, Philadelphia, Pittsburgh, St. Louis, Washington, D.C., and Minneapolis. Chicago was experiencing the worst epidemic in its history. According to the *New York Times*, the Chicago City Health Department claimed that "the first year of the new century will be known as the typhoid fever year."[30] Between 1891 and 1910, Minneapolis suffered an average of 950 cases of typhoid fever per year, and about 10 percent, or ninety-five people, died from it each year.[31]

Beginning in 1880, soldiers at Fort Snelling constructed a waterworks system that delivered fresh water from Coldwater Spring to the quickly expanding Upper Post (which now lies adjacent to the Minneapolis–St. Paul International Airport). So it is puzzling that during the Spanish-American War (1898), Minnesota used the Minnesota State Fairgrounds as a temporary camp rather than mustering and training them at Fort Snelling. The choice proved deadly for the Fifteenth Minnesota Volunteer Infantry.

The young men came from the Twin Cities and from Worthington, Willmar, Luverne, and other towns around the state. Before leaving Worthington, the city threw their volunteers a great "feast and fete at the Court House Park where tables and trees were lighted by hundreds of electric lights especially for the occasion," says Ray Crippen.[32] The men arrived at the state fairgrounds on July 5 and 6. On July 18, the whole Fifteenth Regiment, 1,326 men, "a larger number than had ever before been mobilized in the state under one organization," was mustered into the U.S. Army.[33] But by July 30, the United States and Spain had already begun negotiating a cease-fire, so the soldiers stayed and trained at Camp Ramsey, at the state fairgrounds, in St. Paul. It must have been a festive place for the young soldiers. Family, friends, and the curious continually visited the camp. Out-

FIGURE 6.3 » Troop review at Camp Ramsey, 1898, the Minnesota State Fairgrounds. Courtesy of Minnesota Historical Society.

of-town visitors arrived on the weekends by excursion trains. Tell Turner, the regiment's chaplain, remembered, "There was a gala season for each day" and "From four o'clock until dark the camp was a veritable Fair Ground."[34]

Some of the new recruits reported to sick call each morning complaining of sore feet, upset stomachs, or other temporary maladies. Late July and early August had been tropical, making some think of Cuba, Puerto Rico, or the Philippines, where they might have been headed. Seventy-five men reported for sick call on July 16, but Turner says the doctors suspected that the men had been drinking too much water, due to the heat. A couple of days later, the camp hospital had emptied out. Some soldiers had reported to sick call, Turner admitted, to get out of the day's drilling. The heat continued, and the men kept pouring down the water.[35]

On July 25 some men reported to sick call whose condition worried the doctors. Unlike those trying to escape the daily drills, these patients did not get better; their symptoms grew worse over the next few days. Tests of the water on July 27 located the typhoid bacilli in one specimen taken from the regiment's water supply tank, suggesting this had been the source. Some doctors were not convinced yet, but by August 6 the regimental hospital had eighteen critical cases, all confirmed as typhoid. On August 12, the United States and Spain signed a peace protocol ending most combat. By August 16, 178 men from the Fifteenth Minnesota had reported sick and area hospitals had admitted 45. Chaplain Turner recorded, "There were not enough ambulances in the two cities to meet the Requirements and street cars had to be put into service." By August 21, "new victims were succumbing at a rate of 20 per day." Colonel H. A. Leonhauser wired the war department and pleaded for permission to move his regiment to Fort Snelling and received quick approval. On August 23 the Fifteenth Minnesota marched to the fort, with its clean water supply.[36]

Men continued to fall sick, but the epidemic finally began subsiding in mid-September. In all, it claimed eighteen lives. Area hospitals cared for 360 men and another 40 were hospitalized in Chicago and in Philadelphia, Harrisburg, and Reading, Pennsylvania, after the regiment left Fort Snelling for Camp Mead, Pennsylvania. Most patients remained sick for about seventy days.[37]

The Army sent Dr. Walter Reed and a board of u.s. Army surgeons to Minneapolis to investigate the cause. Dr. Reed had helped defeat yellow fever and had made dealing with typhoid a priority. The investigators traced the epidemic's source "to the 'notoriously infected water' supply of the City of Minneapolis." Minneapolis had experienced over three thousand typhoid cases the year before, which the investigators speculated may have been related. On December 10, 1898, the United States and Spain signed the Treaty of Paris, ending the war. The Army did not need the Fifteenth Regiment of Minnesota Volunteers. They had fought their toughest battle and suffered their worst casualties without ever leaving the country.[38]

Closer to the I-35W bridge site, the west side immigrant community of Bohemian Flats lived in everyday contact with the river. Their homes lay tucked below the bluff on a small floodplain that wrapped around the bend below the bridge site. Established about 1880, the community counted 1,200 residents by 1900, of a variety of ethnic backgrounds. They sank wells deep into the sand. While often clean and clear, each time the river flooded, polluted waters from the Mississippi filled the wells. After a typhoid epidemic at Bohemian Flats in 1900, the city closed the wells and provided city water.[39]

Among the immigrants on the flats lived Andrew Kolesar. He arrived from Slovakia in 1891 at the age of twenty-one and quickly rose to become the community's leader.[40] He learned how to play Minneapolis politics and represented the interests of his fellow immigrants at City Hall. The *Minneapolis Tribune* claimed, "In politics the sway of the young man was unquestioned; in family disputes his word was high law; in a social way he was the lion; in business he was a careful and safe adviser." Through his intellect and personal skills, he acquired the job of assistant fireman at the waterworks in Columbia Heights, "the highest position held by any Slovak immigrant in the City of Minneapolis."[41]

Between his job and living on Bohemian Flats, Andrew Kolesar was continually exposed to the Mississippi River's water. In early

FIGURE 6.4 » Bohemian Flats with the Northern Pacific bridge under construction, 1880. Photograph by Emil Hilgarde. Courtesy of Minnesota Historical Society.

March 1902 he contracted typhoid fever and died on March 14 at thirty-two years of age. He was buried in the Minneapolis Pioneers and Soldiers Memorial Cemetery, along with over eight hundred others who died of the fever and are buried there.[42]

DEFEATING TYPHOID

As typhoid fever cases mounted around the country and the world, public health officials began researching ways to combat the disease and discover its origins. In 1880 German bacteriologist Karl Joseph Eberth identified a bacillus he suspected as the cause of typhoid fever.

In 1884, Georg Theodor Gaffky, another German, isolated the bacterium and affirmed Eberth's theory. Many experts, however, did not agree on what transmitted *Salmonella typhi* into humans or what role it played in urban water supply and sanitary treatment.[43] In a *Minneapolis Tribune* article published during the 1897 epidemic in Minneapolis, Dr. H. H. Kimball said the polluted streets had caused the disease to spread and claimed that many cases of typhoid were confused with "la grippe," or the flu. In the same article, Dr. Charles Weston, city physician, pointed out that he had looked at forty cases and all had been confirmed as typhoid. Everyone, he said, had been drinking city water, although he admitted that wells could be responsible too.[44] In an article the next day, Dr. Henry Avery, the city's health commissioner, insisted that water was the source of typhoid and that a person had to take it into their stomach to catch the infection. He noted that it could not be breathed in, except maybe through the mouth. Dr. Charles F. Disen, however, offered that typhoid was not contagious but infectious. "It is infectious," he lectured, "in that it may be contracted from bad odors that arise from anything in a stagnant or decayed condition."[45] The *Minneapolis Tribune* presented all the theories as legitimate.

Two methods emerged to eliminate typhoid from urban water supplies, but Minneapolis delayed choosing either. The first was filtration. Poughkeepsie, New York, built the first slow sand filter plant in 1872, but only to improve the smell and taste of the water and to make it look clearer. Not until more than twenty years later did the Lawrence Experiment Station, in Lawrence, Massachusetts, discover that a properly designed slow sand filter could reduce the typhoid bacteria. In 1893 the station built a filter for Lawrence, and the typhoid fever mortality rate plummeted.[46] About twenty cities had slow sand filters by 1900, and by 1910, 28 percent of the urban population in America drank filtered water.[47] Yet in 1904 the taxpayers of Minneapolis rejected a $1 million bond proposal to immediately fund a sand filtration system despite experiencing one of its worst typhoid epidemics that year.[48] Minneapolis would pay a much higher cost in 1910.

On September 26, 1908, Jersey City, New Jersey, became the first city in the United States to permanently chlorinate its water. It already had a sand filtration system. The combination largely eliminated typhoid fever from the city.[49] Chemically treating the water with chlorine may have been too new for Minneapolis to consider. The city's proponents of Mississippi River water wanted to evaluate a number of chemical treatments. Four years earlier, Frank Castner and James Duryea, the two Minneapolis aldermen against a sand filtration system, said that the government had recommended "sulphate of copper" as a way to kill the typhoid bacteria and that St. Louis had been using it successfully.[50] So Minneapolis continued studying the alternatives.

DEBATE AND DELAY

People in Minneapolis had been arguing since the late 1860s over where to get their water. One person had suggested pumping water from a nearby lake (Lake Calhoun) to a reservoir by the river and then distributing it to the city.[51] But Minneapolis had opted for the most abundant and most available source: the Mississippi River; at that time the water was not as polluted as it would become. Outrage against the city water system would grow with the river's increasing pollution and the frequency and severity of typhoid epidemics.

Beginning in early 1909, city planners debated the potential sources and costs of acquiring clean water. Sand filters had already proven themselves, but taxpayers were not ready to commit over $1 million to build one. They hoped for a cheaper option and were willing to take their time. Responding to demands from businesses and social and professional organizations, Minneapolis established a Pure Water Commission. The commission evaluated four options: continued use of the river but with some kind of filtration and/or chemical treatment; deep wells; a pipeline to Mille Lacs Lake, in central Minnesota; or a pipeline to Lake Superior.[52]

On March 2, 1909, water experts testified before the commission regarding the city's water supply. They told the commission that "they never drank it, would not think of drinking it, and would not recommend anyone else to drink it." They insisted, however, that with filtration, the water could be made "safe and satisfactory for human consumption." But the city had reached its bonding limit, and an act by the state legislature or a two-thirds majority of the city's voters was needed to gain approval to exceed the limit. The voters had not only turned down such a proposal in 1904, they did it again in 1906. Support for state action had not yet jelled.[53]

On June 16 the Pure Water Commission issued its report, with majority and minority opinions. The commissioners ruled out a deep well system. At best it could only supplement the city's supply, and the water was too hard for domestic and commercial use. They also dismissed Lake Superior: it was too far away and its elevation too much lower than Minneapolis, and the costs of the pipeline and pumping stations would have been prohibitive. The commissioners also pointed out that Chicago had moved its water intake farther and farther into Lake Michigan as pollution near the shore increased. Here, agreement ended.[54]

The majority detailed its objections to Mille Lacs Lake. Wind-driven waves over the shallow, 199-square-mile lake stirred up sediment, making the water turbid and killing large numbers of fish, which rotted along the shores. During the late summer and fall, evaporation exceeded rainfall, and the lake had a small watershed. Over two thousand people lived around the lake, explaining why 50 percent of the water samples taken from the lake contained fecal bacteria. Some people living in the drainage area had contracted typhoid fever, and their wastes probably flowed into the lake. A pipeline would cost $6.5 to $8.5 million, and given the water's turbidity and bacterial pollution, it would have to be filtered. In addition, the city would have to buy two hundred feet of shoreline around the lake and all the waterpower rights on the Rum River, which drained out of Mille Lacs. Even without these issues, a battle loomed with the residents around Mille Lacs. Four counties, including eleven small town sites or resort areas, circled the lake. The city would have to convince the state legislature to condemn the land needed. One landowner told the commissioners during a visit to the lake, "'If Minneapolis tries to come to

Mille Lacs Lake for its water you will have the biggest fight you ever saw.'"[55] The minority ignored the threat and criticisms and insisted on more studies.[56]

Mille Lacs remained a candidate, and the city's water commission planned a trip in August to inspect the lake. At a July 23 meeting, Mille Lacs supporter and attorney James A. Peterson accused the filtration backers of being "catspaws" and claimed that they planned to get the filtration plant into private hands, which led to a strong rebuke by some committee members. Joseph Chapman Jr., the commission's chairman, contended that Mille Lacs Lake also had the colon bacillus in it and, denouncing Peterson, proclaimed, "We are not drinking sewer water in Minneapolis and I think it a crime for any citizen to get on the housetop and tell the world we are." Some on the committee had visited nineteen cities and found filtration working. The majority, he pointed out, were not advocating for a full filtration plant but purification by whatever means worked best and for a test filtration system.[57]

The visit to Mille Lacs apparently convinced most commission members that it would not work. By October 2 the Mille Lacs source, although not dead, had lost most of its backers. Still, the city council voted to hire an expert to study the Mississippi and Mille Lacs as water sources and make recommendations on which was best and how the water might be treated.[58]

Winter came and the new year with no resolution, but there were hints of an emerging epidemic. On January 31, 1910, Richard Beard replied to a *Minneapolis Morning Tribune* editorial that declared anyone who carelessly used Minneapolis water was suicidal. Beard went further. He insisted such people were homicidal, for they unwittingly or carelessly transmitted the disease to others, like Typhoid Mary. While critical of individuals, Beard blamed cities that did not filter their water even more. Only filtration, he said, purified the water, and he called for the citizens to demand action from the city council.[59]

By February the epidemic was spreading. On February 24, Joseph Chapman Jr. resigned as head of the Finance Committee for the Board of Charities and Corrections. He blamed the city for the growing epidemic and demanded that the hospitals care for all the sick. The city hospital pleaded that it had no open beds and all the other hospitals were full. The city did not have the funds to hire thirty more nurses but was planning to rent space to house the sick.[60]

Three days later, the *Minneapolis Morning Tribune* published an editorial with the headline "Can Cities Dispense Poison with Impunity?" The editorial suggested legal action against the city. Cities, the *Tribune* declared, were "morally responsible for the spread of infection through public utilities at least." If they could prevent the spread of disease by police action, they had a responsibility to do so. "The *Tribune* always has believed," the editorial asserted, "that a sound construction of the law would make cities legally as well as morally responsible for sickness and death that result from their parsimony, negligence or indifference to human life." Some people tried to ascribe the disease and deaths to an act of God, the *Tribune* chided. "The truth," it said, "is that sickness and death by typhoid fever, in cities whose water supply is impure, are the result of governmental negligence as culpable as the medieval poisoning of wells." The "average juror," the *Tribune* felt, would agree.[61]

At a meeting on March 10, someone asked Dr. P. M. Hall, the city's health commissioner, if the city was suffering an epidemic. His answer left no doubt. Since January 1, he reported, over four hundred people had contracted typhoid and forty-five had died. On March 14, Dr. H. W. Hill of the state health board placed the number of infected at between eight hundred and twelve hundred.[62] And two days later, the *Tribune* no longer hinted at suing the city. Its editorial that day carried the headline "Will Somebody Please Sue the City."[63]

The suit did not come. Minneapolis had acted. In mid-February, the city began building a temporary sterilization plant at Pumping Station No. 4 in Fridley and on February 25 started adding hyperchloride of lime (chlorine) to its water supply. Almost immediately, the treatment destroyed the typhoid bacilli in the two large reservoirs and in the distribution system.[64] This success (and maybe the talk of lawsuits) ended the debate and the delays. Rudolph Herring, a national water expert, convinced Minneapolis to begin construction on a new filtration plant. On January 10, 1913, the Columbia Heights purification plant opened. As Herring recommended, it combined rapid mechanical filtration with coagulation and chlorination.[65] Like other cities around the country, the infection and death rate from typhoid quickly fell.

Surprisingly, in 1935, another epidemic struck Minneapolis, infecting about 190 people and causing six deaths. Investigators traced the source to the Columbia Heights plant. For some reason, the plant had lowered the amount of chlorine it was adding to the water.[66] Obviously, the highly polluted Mississippi River still contained the typhoid bacilli, and only chlorination held it at bay. Except for this incident, Minneapolis appeared free of typhoid. In 1997 *Life* magazine declared, "The filtration of drinking water plus the use of chlorine is probably the most significant public health advance of the millennium."[67]

A GREEN LIGHT TO POLLUTION

More so than any other factor, pollution turned people away from the Mississippi River. They did not just ignore the river—they spurned it. Once the chlorination and subsequent purification methods eliminated waterborne disease and parasites, people could much more easily forget where their water came from. In a generation or two, they forgot the typhoid epidemics, but they did not forget that the river was polluted.

The success of filtration and chlorination helped end a debate between public health officials and sanitary engineers, to the Mississippi's loss. During the first one and a half decades of the twentieth century, a national debate boiled between the public health community and sanitary engineers over sewage treatment and water treatment. Samuel Dixon of Pennsylvania and H. W. Hill of Minnesota were the leading voices of the national public health community arguing against the pollution of rivers and streams and advocating "the ethos of the 'New Public Health.'" Many sanitary engineers who worked for or consulted with cities argued that building separate sanitary and storm sewers and treating the sewage would cost too much. Shifting the responsibility downstream, they held that rivers could purify themselves, and if not, downstream cities could filter and purify their water. They insisted that treating the water through filtration and chlorination was far cheaper than having big cities build sewage treatment plants. By 1914, the sanitary engineers had won out nationally and in Minneapolis. So the city steadily increased the volume of sewage it poured into the Mississippi River.[68]

In 1930, Judson Wicks, the president of the Minnesota Izaak Walton League, estimated that the Twin Cities' 1,100 and 1,200 miles of sewers put 144 million gallons of sewage into the river each day. When these sewers flowed full and the river fell to its low-water stage, 5.8 gallons of water had to dilute one gallon of sewage.[69] So Clarence Jonk should not have been surprised by the pollution when, in 1933, he launched his houseboat into the Mississippi about one-half river mile below today's I-35W bridge site. He had hoped to find inspiration for his writing. He did. More powerfully than any statistics, he captured the impact of pollution. "The Betsy-Nell," he wrote, "has been lowered into the sewage-laden water where fish die, bloat and turn idly about in the eddies, showing their worm-infested bodies like a curse to the men who infected their world. Continuously their white mouths nudge the manure of humanity, the off-wash of the streets and gutters; and here, curling under our starboard side, a brown foam bubbles and steams. Such is our baptism into the Great River."[70] Like so many Mississippi River travel accounts, Jonk's helps us remember what about the river mattered and what did not.

Forgetting and Remembering

The day after the I-35W bridge collapsed, a national television station asked Paul Labovitz, the superintendent of the Mississippi National River and Recreation Area, a unit of the National Park Service, to comment on the Mississippi's water quality at the bridge site. They expected that a dangerously polluted river might add something to the story. When he told them the river was not terribly polluted, they lost interest.[71] The river and the city's relationship with it have come a long way since the early 1900s. The city and the nation have addressed the worst pollution, and people have forgotten the typhoid epidemics. The Eastman Tunnel had also been forgotten, at least until the late 1990s. Now, the Corps of Engineers is telling this story at the Upper St. Anthony Falls Lock and Dam, and Minneapolis is doing so at Water Power Park on Hennepin Island. The Mill City Museum and Mill Ruins Park mark the importance of milling to the city's birth. Society has chosen to forget the one and celebrate the other. The I-35w bridge collapse is different from the Eastman Tunnel failure and the typhoid epidemics in important ways, ways that may make forgetting about it easier.

The I-35w bridge disaster happened instantly, and the rebuilding was remarkably fast. Compared to the Eastman Tunnel and the typhoid epidemics, it was a flash on the historical time line. No events or arguments preceded it, and no drawn-out controversy or debate delayed the fix. The Eastman Tunnel debacle began with the threat of a lawsuit, and construction had been underway for over a year when the tunnel failed. Also, the Eastman Tunnel captured the public's attention for seven years, from 1869 to 1876. The day of the bridge collapse, August 1, 2007, until September 14, 2008, when the new bridge opened, spanned just thirteen and a half months, allowing most people to get on with their lives and back to their old routines. Typhoid fever ravaged the city for decades and debate over an appropriate solution delayed the construction of a water treatment system that would have reduced the number of infections and deaths.

Minneapolis did not depend on the I-35w bridge in 2007 as it did on St. Anthony Falls in 1869 or as it did on the river as a water source from 1871 to 1910. St. Anthony Falls was the economic engine that drove the Minneapolis milling industry, an industry that was the basis of the city's existence and rapid growth. That growth demanded a large water supply. The complete loss of either the falls or the water supply would have been far more than an inconvenience. In both cases the Mississippi River was a vital element of the story. It was not with the bridge disaster.

The riverbed's collapse at St. Anthony Falls focused attention on the Mississippi River. Here the river itself was broken. Although the bridge collapse put cars and victims in the river, requiring rescue and recovery, the bridge collapse was about the bridge. Most news reports simply mentioned the Mississippi as the river the bridge fell into. The event was not about the Mississippi. The Eastman Tunnel failure was directly tied to the river. Once the Corps of Engineers completed the cutoff wall under the Mississippi, the milling industry resumed its rise to national significance. River water turned the mill wheels and saws, and no one could forget what the river meant to Minneapolis. Just the opposite occurred with the I-35W bridge. The government had to get the I-35W bridge rebuilt fast so people could zip over the river again. As long as it remained out, the detours and disruptions reminded people of the tragedy and that the river existed. Now that it is rebuilt, people can forget about both much more easily.

Bridges are about not having to deal with rivers. By crossing over a river on a bridge, people do not have to think about how far down it is, how steep the banks are, how fast the water is flowing, or how deep it is. They do not have to consider how clean or dirty it might be, or whether it is fit for aquatic or human life. The Great River entered a person's life for only seconds when crossing the old I-35W bridge, if they were aware of it at all. Only when the bridge fell into the river did these aspects become relevant.

Few stories reveal more about Minneapolis's early relationship with the Mississippi River than the history of water supply and pollution. It represented a deep need and a deeper disregard. The city needed the river as a water source and as a sewer. For those who used the river's water, it was a constant presence. Water lines delivered the river into homes and businesses throughout the city, continually and repeatedly exposing people to it, and people took it into their bodies when drinking it and when eating food made with it. Before chlorination and filtration, people who consumed river water could tell by the novelty of running water and by the taste and smell. Even more so, they knew by their own experience and the experiences of their families, friends, and coworkers who had become ill or who had died from drinking it.

The number of people sickened and killed by the typhoid epidemics was far greater than those who were injured or died in the I-35W bridge collapse. Thirteen people lost their lives to the bridge collapse and 145 were injured. Between 1871 and 1910, the river's water sickened tens of thousands and killed thousands. This does not include the number infected with parasites and other maladies. Yet society has forgotten about these people and the young soldiers of the Fifteenth Minnesota Volunteer Infantry and Andrew Kolesar of Bohemian Flats. Today, about five hundred thousand people receive Mississippi River water from the Minneapolis waterworks and many do not even know it.[72]

It is surprising how quickly people have forgotten stories that threatened the city's economic foundation and involved tremendous loss of human life. What chance does the I-35W bridge collapse have of being long remembered? Will it be only the site of another tragedy along the Mississippi's banks, or will it be something more? Will it be another place along the Mississippi River intimately tied to the national narrative and the Long Adventure of the Great River? The I-35W bridge collapse, however, has something the other two do not that may ensure its story will last in the local and national memory.

A key contrast between the old I-35W bridge and the new one is that the city and many citizens who participated in the design process wanted a bridge worthy of the Mississippi River and wanted people to know they were crossing the river. They made an intentional effort to reject the idea that a bridge inherently disconnects people from a river. They voted for open railings so motorists could catch a glimpse of the river as they sped across. They pushed for and considered many options for the gateway monuments on top of the bridge to mark the river's presence below. Water ran off the old bridge into the Mississippi, but now it is directed toward drainage ponds. The abutments incorporate native limestone to match the original bluffs. The design includes viewing platforms at the base of the main piers on either side of the river, which provide a spectacular opportunity to view the river at this location. People can watch towboats, motorboats, canoes, and kayaks entering and exiting the Lower St. Anthony Falls Lock and Dam. This feature provides one of the strongest ways for the public to connect with the river. The Department of Trans-portation has agreed to put signs for the Mississippi National River and Recreation Area on the bridge to show that the bridge lies within a unit of the National Park Service focused on the Great River. In all of this, the city and state demonstrated a growing reverence for the Mississippi River.[73]

This is a good start, but how quickly will the sculpture and the signs become a blur in our daily rushes over the river and through our lives? To be remembered, the I-35W bridge site has to rise beyond the story of a local tragedy to one that informs and helps explain the American narrative.

In many respects the I-35W bridge collapse has already achieved a place in the national story line. Within days of the disaster, federal authorities ordered inspectors to examine bridges across the nation and announced a review of the National Bridge Inspection Program "to ensure that Washington is being rigorous in monitoring state inspections."[74] Some states, including Minnesota, closed bridges until thorough inspections could be completed. Barack Obama and other presidential candidates repeatedly used the I-35W bridge failure dur-ing the presidential campaign. President Obama mentioned it specif-ically during his first State of the Union speech, promising to spend $20 billion per year to reduce the number of bridges designated as structurally deficient. And on February 14, 2009, the president signed a $787 million economic stimulus bill that included a large package for roads and bridges. If historians look back at the I-35W bridge col-lapse as the tipping point that forced America to deal with its mas-sive infrastructure repair needs, then the bridge site and the new bridge will certainly become part of the American narrative. And if travelers on the Mississippi photograph it, write about it, and post it in their blogs, Facebook messages, and YouTube videos, the I-35W bridge story will become part of America's Long Adventure with the Great River.

NOTES

1. Clarence Jonk, *River Journey* (repr., St. Paul: Minnesota Historical Society Press, Borealis Books, 2003; New York: Stein and Day, 1964), 58.

2. For the best overview of the history of milling at St. Anthony Falls, see Lucile M. Kane, *The Falls of St. Anthony: The Waterfall That Built Minneapolis* (St. Paul: Minnesota Historical Society Press, 1987), originally published as *The Waterfall That Built a City: The Falls of St. Anthony in Minneapolis* (St. Paul: Minnesota Historical Society Press, 1966); John O. Anfinson, *River of History: A Historic Resources Study of the Mississippi National River and Recreation Area* (St. Paul: U.S. Army Corps of Engineers, 2003), chapter 6.

3. Richard W. Ojakangas and Charles L. Matsch, *Minnesota's Geology* (Minneapolis: University of Minnesota Press, 1982), 75; Merlin H. Berg, "Abstract of Available Historical Data on St. Anthony Falls" (St. Paul District, Corps of Engineers Records, ca. 1939), 1–3.

4. Berg, "Abstract of Available Historical Data," 4; Kane, *The Falls of St. Anthony*, 70–72.

5. Kane, *The Falls of St. Anthony*, 71–72; *Minneapolis Tribune*, October 6, 1869.

6. Kane, *The Falls of St. Anthony*, 69–70; Berg, "Abstract of Available Historical Data," 4.

7. Berg, "Abstract of Available Historical Data," 6–9. A cofferdam is a dam built to create a work site in a river. Once complete, the water is pumped out and the riverbed is exposed.

8. Ibid., 8–9.

9. Ibid., 9–10. The cutoff wall formed a dam under the riverbed. It cut off the flow of water through the sandstone, thereby stopping the falls' collapse.

10. Ibid., 10–14.

11. Quoted in Kane, *The Falls of St. Anthony*, 79.

12. Berg, "Abstract of Available Historical Data," 10–16; Kane, *The Falls of St. Anthony*, 77–79.

13. Rufus J. Baldwin, chapter 24, "Water Works," in *History of the City of Minneapolis, Minnesota, Part II*, ed. Isaac Atwater (New York: Munsell & Company, 1893), 805.

14. Between 1867 and 1868, the city put a Holly pump into a building on the west side, but the pump was primarily for fighting fires. The mill became known as the Holly Mill for the pump. See "The Water Works of the City of Minneapolis Minnesota: A Brief Historical Sketch of the Present Water Works (January First 1919)," p. 3, Minnesota Historical Society Collections.

15. Baldwin, "Water Works," 806. There is some disagreement on the starting dates for the waterworks. Baldwin (ibid.) says that Minneapolis built its first waterworks in 1871. "The Water Works of the City of Minneapolis" says, "The first regular installation was made in 1872 at Station No. 1, located at the foot of Fifth Avenue South and the Mississippi River, above the falls" (3).

16. "The Water Works of the City of Minneapolis," 3, 5.

17. James A. Dodge, C. L. Herrick, and C. W. Hall, "Paper C, Water Supply of Minneapolis—Committee (March 6, 1883)," 38–44, quote, 41, emphasis in original, Minnesota Historical Society Collections.

18. Baldwin, "Water Works," 807; "The Water Works of the City of Minneapolis," 5.

19. Baldwin, "Water Works," 807.

20. Ibid.

21. Ibid.

22. "The Water Works of the City of Minneapolis" explains that "all pumping was made direct to the distribution system until 1897 when two reservoir basins at Columbia Heights were completed" (5). The *Minneapolis Tribune* announced when filling of the reservoirs had begun (March 17, 1897, and December 30, 1897).

23. "The Water Works of the City of Minneapolis," 5, 7.

24. Rudolph D. Herring, "Report on an Improved Water Supply for the City of Minneapolis, March 17, 1910," 22, Minnesota Historical Society Collections.

25. Joel Tarr, James McCurley, and Terry F. Yosie, "The Development and Impact of Urban Wastewater Technology: Changing Concepts of Water Quality Control, 1850–1930," in *Pollution and Reform in American Cities, 1870–1930*, ed. Martin Melosi (Austin: University of Texas, 1980), 60-62.

26. Tarr et. al., "Development and Impact of Urban Wastewater Technology," 63-69.

27. "History of Stormwater and Wastewater Drainage Systems in Minneapolis," http://www.ci.minneapolis.mn.us/stormwater/overview/construction-history.asp.

28. Baldwin, "Water Works," 806.

29. Stuart Galishoff, "Triumph and Failure: The American Water Supply Problem, 1860–1923," in Melosi, *Pollution and Reform*, 33-40.

30. *New York Times*, October 15, 1901.

31. "Report of Investigations of the Typhoid Fever Epidemic Minneapolis, 1935," Minnesota Department of Health, 1938, 95.

32. Ray Crippen, "The Misfortune of Company H, Nobles County, Minnesota, 1898 . . . About the sickest military outfit you could ever imagine," Spanish-American War Centennial Web site, http://www.spanamwar.com/15thMinnCoH.htm.

33. T. A. Turner, *Story of the Fifteenth Minnesota Volunteer Infantry* (Minneapolis: Lessard Printing Company, 1899), quote, 22; see chapter 2, "Assembling and Organizing."

34. Ibid., quote, 28; see also 27-28.

35. Ibid., 24-26.

36. Ibid., 36-37; *Minneapolis Tribune*, August 10, 1898; *Minneapolis Tribune*, August 11, 1898; *Minneapolis Tribune*, August 22, 1898. The *Minneapolis Tribune*, August 23, 1898, reported, "At about the hour of 4 o'clock yesterday afternoon a special car on the Como interurban carried another load of 33 soldiers of the 15th Minnesota regiment to the Minneapolis hospitals."

37. Ibid., 38-39.

38. Crippen, "The Misfortune of Company H." See also Walter Reed, Victor Vaughn, and Edward O. Shakespeare, *Report on the Origin and Spread of Typhoid Fever during the Spanish War of 1898*, vol. 1 (Washington, D.C.: Government Printing Office, 1904); see p. 424 on the "notoriously" bad water and p. 426 on the estimate of three thousand typhoid cases in Minneapolis in 1897.

39. *The Bohemian Flats*, compiled by the workers of the Writer's Program of the Works Projects Administration in the State of Minnesota (repr., St. Paul: Minnesota Historical Society Press, 1986; Minneapolis: University of Minnesota Press, 1941).

40. *Minneapolis Tribune*, March 16, 1902; "Respected and Trusted Bohemian Ally, Andrew Kolesar, Dies of Typhoid Fever," Minneapolis Pioneers and Soldiers Memorial Cemetery History Page, Alley Article, http://www.friendsofthecemetery.org/history/alley_articles/ kolesar_andrew.shtml.

41. *Minneapolis Tribune*, March 16, 1902. The article says he worked at the pumping station in northeast Minneapolis, but the pumping station was in Fridley.

42. Ibid.; Minneapolis Pioneers and and Soldiers Memorial Cemetery History Page.

43. Hans P. Riemann and Dean O. Cliver, *Foodborne Infections and Intoxications*, 3rd ed. (San Diego, Calif.: Academic Press, 2006), 58.

44. *Minneapolis Tribune*, March 26, 1897.

45. *Minneapolis Tribune*, March 27, 1897.

46. Massachusetts Department of Environmental Protection, http://www.mass.gov/dep/ about/organization/early4.htm. According to Tarr et. al., in "Development and Impact of Urban Wastewater Technology," "The typhoid fever mortality rate in Lawrence dropped from an average of about 120 per 100,000 population in the years 1887-92 to an annual rate of between 20 and 30" (44-45).

47. Tarr et al., "Development and Impact of Urban Wastewater Technology," 45, 73.

48. Frank H. Castner and James H. Duryea, "Pure Water for Minneapolis," 1905, 1-7, Minnesota Historical Society Collections.

49. "A Giant Step for Public Health: Chlorination in Chicago and Jersey City," http://www .americanchemistry.com/100years/CityHistory.html; Galishoff, "Triumph and Failure," 45.

50. Castner and Duryea, "Pure Water for Minneapolis," 2.

51. Baldwin, "Water Works," 805-6.

52. "Report of Pure Water Commission," Minneapolis, Minnesota, July 16, 1909, Minnesota Historical Society Collections.

53. *Minneapolis Morning Tribune*, March 2, 1909.

54. "Report of Pure Water Commission," 1-3.

55. Ibid., 10.

56. Ibid., 2-3, 5-10.

57. *Minneapolis Morning Tribune*, July 23, 1909.

58. *Minneapolis Morning Tribune*, October 10, 1909.

59. *Minneapolis Morning Tribune*, January 31, 1910.

60. *Minneapolis Morning Tribune*, February 24, 1910.

61. *Minneapolis Morning Tribune*, February 27, 1910.

62. *Minneapolis Morning Tribune*, March 14, 1910.

63. *Minneapolis Morning Tribune*, March 16, 1910. In this article, Dr. Hall added, "The present epidemic is the first in the history of the city to come through the city water from outside the city. Undoubtedly it comes from Brainerd and towns between here and there." Secondary infections had probably come from wells, he thought.

64. Herring, "Report on an Improved Water Supply," 10.

65. Ibid., 26–27. According to "The Water Works of the City of Minneapolis," the new plant "consisted of a 75,000,000-gallon sedimentation basin, head house, mixing chamber, two coagulation basins, twelve filter units having a total capacity of 39,000,000 gallons per day, two auxiliary clear water basins, a covered 45,000,000-gallon clear water reservoir and an elevated wash water tank" (15).

66. "Report of Investigations of the Typhoid Fever Epidemic Minneapolis, 1935," 95.

67. "The World as It Was—And the Events That Changed It," *Life* magazine, Fall 1997, 80.

68. Tarr et. al., "Development and Impact of Urban Wastewater Technology," 72–73.

69. Judson Wicks, "Pollution of the Upper Mississippi River," *Transactions of the American Fisheries Society* 60 (1930): 287–92.

70. Jonk, *River Journey*, 79.

71. Paul Labovitz, personal communication, August 2, 2007.

72. City of Minneapolis, Water Department, Minneapolis Water Facts, http://www .ci.minneapolis.mn.us/water/waterfacts.asp. St. Paul also draws water from the Mississippi and supplies about 417,000 people with river water in St. Paul and suburbs. "Sustainable St. Paul," http://mn-stpaul.civicplus.com/DocumentView.asp?DID=1494, p. 12.

73. Steve P. Johnson, chief of resource management, Mississippi National River and Recreation Area, personal communication, March 2009. Mr. Johnson attended many of the design meetings for the new bridge.

74. Matthew L. Wald and Kenneth Chang, *New York Times*, August 4, 2007.

CHAPTER SEVEN

A Bridge to Somewhere

Mark Pedelty, Heather Dorsey, and Melissa Thompson

Imagine a Minneapolis bridge. Perhaps a concrete jumble comes to mind, along with televised images of courageous rescue workers helping survivors get out of the river and their ruined cars. However, this chapter is not about that bridge, it is about a different one just a mile downstream. It is about a time before the I-35W bridge collapse. It is about the dramatic efforts of a small group of students trying to get a community to start noticing its river, to start taking care of its river. It is not about disconnections—broken bridges and policy failures—it is about connections, connections between individuals, communities, rivers, and oceans. Specifically, this chapter is about the Bridge Project, an event involving performing students, passing audiences, a campus, and a community.

Unfortunately, the story is not just a celebration. There is a tragic element to this bridge story as well, involving polluted stormwater runoff in urban Minnesota, algae blooms in the Gulf of Mexico, and millions of dead fish. Over two thousand miles downriver from Minneapolis, a phenomenon known as the dead zone occurs each year on a cycle that coincides with the agricultural season farther north. Excess nitrates from fertilizers and detritus run into ditches, streams, and rivers feeding into the Mississippi. The nation's major artery takes those nitrates down to the Delta and the Gulf of Mexico, where they feed hungry algae. The algae reproduce and grow out of control. After gobbling up the oxygen, creating in the water a condition known as hypoxia, the algae die, leaving a large area with virtually no life. The dead zone started out being compared to Rhode Island, but a larger state is needed to describe it each year. In 2008 it was the size of New Jersey. "A major dead zone (an area where marine life is stressed because of lack of oxygen) now exists in the Gulf of Mexico along Louisiana and parts of Texas," note G. E. Galloway, D. F. Boesch, and R. R. Twilley, "as a result of excessive nutrients traveling down the Mississippi from the farmland of the Midwest," a stream of pollutants that has "increased threefold since the 1960s" thanks to increasingly intensive and input-dependent farming methods.[1]

The people of Minnesota have no idea that they are destroying an ocean biome. Does that sound a bit too dramatic? Consider the coverage of the bridge collapse, which was repeatedly referred to as a tragedy. Of course, when people die unnecessarily it is indeed tragic, and we do not intend to downplay that tragedy. It was only right that such a spectacular bridge failure would capture the attention of a nation. It sparked a long overdue national dialogue concerning infrastructure. Unfortunately, no such dialogue began concerning river ecology, urban planning, or the most outdated aspect of our infrastructure, cars. Instead of rethinking our energy-intensive way of life, we patted ourselves on the back for the heroic measures taken to quickly restore automobile access.

Tragedy is compounded when nothing is learned from events like the bridge collapse. In the news, meaning was reduced to a tragically bad accident, with some additional discussion of policy failures that may or may not have contributed to the problem. Heroic efforts were taken to get commuters back on the road, to build a better bridge, to get past the tragedy and back to normal. Unfortunately, normal is unsustainable transportation, architecture, and urban planning. The rapid rebuild was presented as a testament to the work ethic of the Midwest. But what does that story really tell us? What does it hide? What more do we need to know? We would suggest that an opportunity to modernize our transportation system, make it more sustainable, and thus alter our relationship to the river was largely lost. We will return to that critique in the conclusion, but first we will reflect on a pedagogical project that may provide us a glimpse of more sustainable futures and how to achieve them.

The Bridge Project described here took place in 2003 through 2006, in the years leading up to the I-35W bridge collapse. It is part of the same story, told in a different way, a story that looked back into history, acknowledged the unsustainable nature of our current system, and imagined a better future. In a course titled "Identity, Community, and Culture in the Performing Arts," University of Minnesota students were given the following assignment: (1) study the Gulf of Mexico dead zone; (2) choose a poem, song, or story about the river; (3) transform the text into a performance about the dead zone; and (4) present the performance on the pedestrian deck of the Washington Avenue bridge. The goal was to make more people aware of the dead zone and our role in exacerbating or ameliorating the problem. The Mississippi River runs through the middle of the University of Minnesota Twin Cities campus, defining both the campus and community. Therefore, the performances had more than a theoretical connection to the problem; they were presented where the campus community encounters our nation's definitive river. This chapter is about those performances. As such, it is also a guide for those who would like to do something like it in their class or community organization.

The Performances

A semester of hard work went into each bridge performance. Because the students knew that they would be performing in public at the end of the semester, they invested great energy and meaning into their learning. For example, Nhia Xiong performed her grandmother's struggle to cross the Mai Kong River in Laos. Nhia translated letters and correspondence that her grandmother sent to relatives detailing

FIGURE 7.1 » Bonnie Nguyen dancing and performing poetry inside the Washington Avenue bridge pedestrian walkway. Photograph by Patrick O'Leary.

the horrors of the evacuation, the harshness of the journey, and the feeling of safety when they finally reached the river. The river meant survival for Nhia's family and the Hmong people. Nhia used traditional Hmong instrumental music as background and wrote lyrics that addressed the refugee's struggles. She wore traditional Hmong dress and carried the parchment from her grandmother's letters.

Bonnie Nguyen also drew on her cultural identities and experiences to forge a connection to the river. She eloquently describes how the class performance was not merely representing existing cultural realities, but also attempting to construct a new one:

When I was told that we had to do an artistic piece relating to the Mississippi River, I was extremely nervous and felt out of my comfort zone. I had no idea what I could do that would be inspirational and convey the importance of the Mississippi River without being too generic. After much thought, I finally was able to dig deeper within my own culture and heritage to come up with a piece called "Mystics of the Mississippi." My piece incorporated traditional Vietnamese dance along with reciting an American poem. After reflecting back on this performance after so many years, I see the true significance of this project. I feel that my piece was a melting pot of who I am as a Vietnamese American living in the community. I felt that my performance, as well as other students' performances, was a combination of all cultures, religions, and heritages coming together to honor the Mississippi River.

Bonnie places the river at the center of a multicultural community, conceiving of it as a special, living entity that provides a sense of shared purpose and unity. The river is something that we should "honor" rather than simply use as a resource, platform, or backdrop.

Kaia Yngre's performance presented a more dystopic vision, more of a reflection of what we are in relation to the river rather than what we could be. She wore a torn, ragged white wedding dress entangled in fish netting. Placed throughout the netting were rusted pop cans, soaked papers, cigarette butts, and other trash. She sang an original song depicting the torment and sadness of a bride left at the altar, alone on her wedding day. Her point was that humans pollute purity and beauty without thinking of the consequences.

In another moving performance, Marcel Withers wrote an original monologue from a slave's point of view, equating the slave's survival with the river's. Marcel incorporated Langston Hughes's classic poem "The Negro Speaks of Rivers." Given the option between either choosing their own poems, songs, or monologues or picking from a list of river-themed pieces compiled beforehand, more students chose Hughes's masterwork than any other text. Each student emphasized a slightly different aspect of "The Negro Speaks of Rivers," such as injustice, transcendence, truth, beauty, hope.

Although the results were remarkable, it was not an easy experience for the students. The majority had never performed in public, so much of the class each semester was spent overcoming inhibitions and learning basic performance techniques. Even those with some experience found the idea of performing solo in a public setting frightening. Focusing on the practical environmental goal of river stewardship seemed to help. Catalina Hotung explains:

> I had never liked performing solo in front of people, so in all honesty I do have to say that my primary concern for a long time was nerves and how I'd get over them in time to pull off the performance. However, as the class progressed, we covered some of the environmental issues that the Mississippi had undergone, and it really opened my eyes to how

FIGURE 7.2 » Catalina Hotung performs "River in the Rain," from the musical *Big River*. Photograph by Patrick O'Leary.

far and destructive damage could be when it was all added together.... The realization of what the dead zone actually was and how it came to be helped motivate me. I was doing something for a greater cause than getting a good grade and through performance we used an alternate, more creative medium for bringing attention to the issue. I remember many people taking time from their routine walk across the bridge to watch us, and on occasion they would try to talk to us to try to delve deeper into our cause. I feel that by performing rather than handing out leaflets we appealed to peoples' curiosity as well as created a comfortable space in which they could break from their schedule and watch us for a bit.

FIGURE 7.3 » Sandi Betz performs on a warm spring day. Authors' photograph.

FIGURE 7.4 » Kalah Smith performing from the fish's perspective. Photograph by Patrick O'Leary.

Catalina reminds us that there are serious obstacles to environmental performance in Minnesota:

> I performed both in the fall and the spring and I must say I found one more effective than the other in bringing awareness to the river. In the spring we were able to perform on the outer part of the bridge rather than the inside, thereby establishing a stronger connection with the river, not to mention it was much warmer and people were more willing to linger for a bit longer.

Kalah Smith argues that public performances like the Bridge Project can build healthier communities:

> The main thing I took from that experience was that giving back to the community can come in many different forms. It was nice to see how just an hour of our time helped de-stress college students during finals week. A lot of people stopped and took the time to listen to our performances. Finals are always stressful, and to see people out there entertaining them as they walked to their next final really seemed to help lighten the mood around campus.
>
> I believe that the performance and performances like that help a community come together. It can inspire people to come out of their shells and get more involved. It's easy to walk around campus listening to your iPod and not talk to other people or notice what's going on around you. However, events like that can help a community start talking and learn how to relate to one another. If nothing else it can

give them something to talk to their neighbor in class about. I honestly did have a lot of fun that day. I was nervous at first, but it was easy to step out of my shell when I saw that a lot of other people enjoyed it.

Teachers reading this might be thinking, "How could I incorporate something like this into my course?" Behind that question there is often a healthy sense of apprehension and doubt that someone

FIGURE 7.5 » The Unknown Turtle seeks donations for Friends of the Mississippi River cleanup projects. Photograph by Patrick O'Leary.

trained as an instructor of a seemingly unrelated subject would also have the necessary skills to integrate performance. The truth is that no instructor has the knowledge and skills necessary for successful performance-based pedagogy. That is the point. The value of the course lies not in the knowledge of the instructor but in the collective experience, energy, and talents of the students. The teacher creates the structure within which the varied talents of students can be brought to bear, a decentered pedagogy whose promise is collectively shared and realized.[2]

The Power of Performance?

We did not formally assess the effectiveness of the performance campaign, nor would such an assessment be possible. The audience was mostly on the move, stopping only for brief periods to catch a performance or two before rushing on to class, work, or home. Even if we could have surveyed the audience, it would be extremely difficult to determine whether or not performance translated into under-

FIGURE 7.6 » Instructor Heather Dorsey leads the students in a performance of "Black River," by William Topley. Photograph by Patrick O'Leary.

standing, understanding into action, and action into environmental improvement. Like performance itself, the campaign was an act of faith and hope, a reasonable belief that when faced with compelling information people will make better decisions. The goal of performance is to capture the audience's attention and intellect through appeals to their sense of aesthetics and emotions. The assumption is that scientific reports measuring the depths of our dystopia are simply not enough to motivate people to think and act.

There is some empirical evidence, however slight, to reinforce that faith. During the last ten years the number of references to the dead zone (those that actually refer to the Gulf of Mexico and not a movie or lack of cell phone coverage) has steadily increased. After an initial splash of attention in 1999, news coverage of the phenomenon virtually disappeared in 2000 and 2001, perhaps coinciding with a political shift away from environmental concerns in 2000 and the 9/11 attacks in 2001. However, steady gains were made each year thereafter. According to an analysis of news reports collected in the LexisNexis database that included "dead zone" in the text, more than twice as many news stories were written about the Gulf dead zone in 2008 as in 1999.

Of course, the pattern of coverage somewhat mirrors the phenomenon itself. As the Gulf dead zone grows, so does press attention. However, the rate of increase of news coverage exceeds the rate of growth of the dead zone itself. Granted, it will take more than forty-nine stories per year in major national media to effectively deal with the problem, but increased attention in the press gives some cause for hope to those who have been involved in public communication efforts.

The press reacts to the agendas of others, from politicians to activists. The combined efforts of thousands of people performing their public roles—biologists, chemists, water management professionals, and environmental activists—are probably having some effect, at least on press attention. Hopefully, that attention will translate into meaningful action and, ultimately, a reduction in the size of the Gulf dead zone.

TABLE 7.1 » News coverage of the Gulf of Mexico dead zone in major U.S. newspapers

Year	Total number of articles mentioning "dead zone"	Number of articles mentioning Gulf phenomenon	Number of articles referring to another topic	Percentage of articles mentioning Gulf phenomenon	Percentage of articles referring to another topic
1999	56	24	32	42.9	57.1
2000	48	1	47	2.0	98.0
2001	48	2	46	4.2	95.8
2002	117	15	102	12.8	87.2
2003	104	11	93	10.6	89.4
2004	137	39	98	28.5	71.5
2005	93	30	63	32.3	67.7
2006	100	31	69	31.0	69.0
2007	104	39	65	37.5	62.5
2008	116	49	67	42.2	57.8

Source: LexisNexis, January 2, 2009

Note: Due to litigation involving freelance news reports, news aggregators like Lexis-Nexis do not have an entirely complete record for certain publications. Therefore, the percentage columns are the best indicators for trends in news coverage.

Conclusion

It is easy to become cynical, watching bridges fall and return without a meaningful change in the way we get around. We pat ourselves on the back for creating ever more ingenious ways to protect ourselves *from* the river, while the failure of each new innovation should remind us just how unsustainable our relationship to the river is. From falling bridges in Minnesota to massive floods in Iowa and levee-destroying hurricanes in Louisiana, the Mississippi River provides empirical evidence that technology alone cannot solve our environmental problems, problems that are as much ideological and institutional as they are material.

The rhetoric around the bridge rebuilding project was predominantly about getting cars moving efficiently once again, about mak-

A BRIDGE TO SOMEWHERE   151

ing sure that the worker-consumers in them and the industries they serve would not be overly inconvenienced by the momentary downturn in productivity. That discourse reflected unquestioned commitment to high consumption and growth, regardless of the environmental consequences. It reflects the great ideological dissonance of our time as material reality makes light of the fantastical logic of consumer capitalism: our belief that unlimited growth and consumption are somehow sustainable. The crumbling infrastructure of high modernism is being replaced by more of the same, only this time shorn of its aesthetic graces. The old bridge was green and brown, melding more effectively into its surroundings. The new bridge is bright white concrete, lit blue and pink at night lest we forget it is there. "This time you will not defeat us!" shouts the new bridge at the old river.

One could view the rebuilding of the I-35W bridge as a triumph, as did the cheering and honking drivers who poured back over the span at 5:00 A.M. on Thursday, September 18, 2008. The time of their commute was reduced, slightly, and at a very great expense. An unsustainable system of transportation was reproduced quickly and with great fanfare. Beyond a few engineering concessions to potential future light rail access, no moves were made to foster better bicycle or foot transportation around the affected area. Bicycle and foot traffic routes under and over each end of the bridge continued largely as they were. Pedestrians and bicyclists on the north end commuting to the University of Minnesota campus must continue to share dangerous high-volume surface streets with cars rushing to get to the bridge, navigating dangerous ramp crossings and traffic lights. All efforts to gain bicycle and foot pathways under the north end of the bridge were ignored in the rush to get the bridge restored.

What would seem to be a natural connection from the historic Stone Arch Bridge to the University of Minnesota campus, passing directly under the I-35W bridge, remains officially off limits to bicyclists and pedestrians for the sake of providing rail and truck access to a coal plant. That coal plant heats the University of Minnesota Twin Cities campus, yet another monument to outdated infrastructure along the Minneapolis riverfront. Repeated efforts to gain a bike and walking pathway under the north end of the bridge have been ignored by the university and actively opposed by the railroad company that supplies the university with its coal and other fuels. In an area that could be the very model of sustainable transition, the interests of local neighborhoods have been ignored in favor of cars, suburban commuters, and a coal plant that generations of Minneapolis activists have sought to remove from the riverfront.

It is easy to become cynical. Fortunately, nothing challenges cynicism better than education and performance. It was impossible to watch the young performers on the Washington Avenue bridge without feeling some hope for the future. Engaged performance not only informs and inspires audiences, it also helps us to imagine new worlds. The performers illustrated here, along with their classmates, provided a glimpse of communities reconnected to rivers, a new world brought to life in the expressive faces, bodies, voices, and vital art of a new generation.

Performance is much more than metaphor. Tragic realities like the Gulf dead zone are created through millions of individual acts each day, performances that are, in turn, defined and circumscribed by large-scale government policies, ideologies, and monumental constructs like the I-35W and Washington Avenue bridges. It takes equally dramatic action to bring rivers, bridges, cities, and oceans back to life. The student performances chronicled here provide some small glimpses into what that sustainable future might look like.

NOTES

1. G. E. Galloway, D. F. Boesch, and R. R. Twilley, "Restoring and Protecting Coastal Louisiana," *Issues in Science and Technology* 25, no. 2 (2009): 29–38, 34.

2. L. Grobman, "Toward a Multicultural Pedagogy: Literary and Nonliterary Traditions," *MELUS* 26, no. 1 (2001): 221.

CHAPTER EIGHT

Old Man River

Deborah L. Swackhamer

Ol' Man River
He must know something
But don't say nothing
He just keeps rolling
He keeps on rolling along.
—Oscar Hammerstein, 1927

The Twin Cities was reminded once again on that fateful August evening in 2007 that the Mighty Mississippi River runs through its core. The I-35W bridge collapse was shocking in many ways, and it was made all the more dramatic by the fact that the nation's largest river was involved in the crossing.

Interstate 35 is one of the major north-south transportation routes in the United States, beginning in Duluth, Minnesota, and running all the way to Laredo, Texas. It is a major artery in the remarkable interstate highway system put in place by President Eisenhower in the late 1950s. It connects a state bordering Canada with one bordering Mexico. It is part of the basic skeletal structure of the country from a human infrastructure perspective. The Mississippi River is its equal from a natural landscape perspective—it is the nation's major water vein, gathering water across the midsection of the country and carrying it to the Gulf of Mexico.

As horrific as the bridge collapse was, the cars, debris, and rescue efforts had little impact on the river itself. Even construction of the new bridge had minimal impact. The river did not care about the human suffering the bridge collapse caused; it just kept rolling, a silent witness of the day.

Typically, the Mississippi River in the Twin Cities is viewed as something one needs to get across. It is a barrier, an obstacle, and most people that cross the river several times a day or week pay little attention to it. Bridges are constructed to get us across rivers, not to experience the river. The river is taken for granted by the vast majority of the local population. The tragedy of the bridge collapse may have had a small positive side benefit by uncovering the river and shining a light on it. It is a remarkable resource, and the remainder of this article will highlight its grandeur, the threats to that grandeur, and our responsibility to maintain its grandeur.

Physical Grandeur—The Mighty Mississippi

The Mississippi River starts as a trickle near Lake Itasca, Minnesota, and then travels 2,340 miles before reaching its great delta south of New Orleans. When one includes its largest tributary, the Missouri River, the river system is 3,900 miles long and is the longest river in North America and the fourth-longest river in the world. It discharges 572,000 cubic feet per second into the Gulf of Mexico, making it the tenth-largest river in the world by volume of flow. It lives up to its Ojibwe name of *misi-ziibi*, or "Great River."

As it flows south, it touches ten states in the heartland of the nation. Perhaps more impressive is that its drainage basin includes thirty-two states, which is equal to about one-third of the area of the entire lower forty-eight states combined. The Missouri River drainage basin and the Ohio River drainage basin are large contributors to this.[1] It drains all of the Corn Belt, the agricultural states that produce much of the world's corn crop. This contributes significantly to its biggest pollution threat, discussed later.

In Minnesota, the scale of the river is equally impressive. The river runs for 575 miles from Lake Itasca to the Iowa border, and it drains 40 percent of the state's surface area. More than three-fourths of the state's population lives within the river's watershed. The state portion of the watershed boasts two national park service units—the Mississippi River National Recreation Area and the St. Croix National Scenic Riverway—as well as a major U.S. Fish and Wildlife Service National Wildlife Refuge.

The Mississippi River and its basin are also critical to the economic well-being of the region and the nation. Commercial navigation, tourism, agriculture production, mineral resources, and energy production all contribute billions of dollars annually to the economy.

Ecological Grandeur—Biodiversity and the Mississippi Flyway

The Mississippi is not just expansive, it is a rich and diverse ecosystem. The Upper Mississippi National Wildlife Refuge is home to more than 600 species of plants, 119 species of fish, 42 species of freshwater mussels, 31 species of reptiles, and 14 species of amphibians. It contains 48,000 acres of marsh habitat, 51,000 acres of floodplain forest, and 5,700 acres of grassland including native prairie. While such habitats are less frequent the farther downstream one moves, there is still a variety of robust ecosystems extending down the entire length of the river.

For example, the Delta National Wildlife Refuge is the southernmost national refuge along the Mississippi, located at the natural mouth of the river about one hundred miles south of New Orleans, Louisiana. Its primary function is to serve as a sanctuary for hundreds of thousands of migratory waterfowl during winter months. Many other refuges along the river have been created, particularly to provide protection of bird habitat.

The Mississippi River is especially rich in waterfowl and migratory birds. In just the Upper Mississippi National Wildlife Refuge alone, one-half of the entire world's canvasback duck population and

20 percent of the eastern population of tundra swans use the river as a staging area for their annual migration. The bald eagle population peaks at 2,700 during their spring migration, and there are 167 bald eagle nests. More than 5,000 great blue heron and common egrets nest in fifteen different colonies.

This extraordinary richness is largely due to what is known as the Mississippi River flyway, the largest of the three major migratory bird pathways between North America and South America.[2] It is the bird equivalent of U.S. Interstate 35. The Mississippi River flyway reaches from above the Arctic Circle in Alaska to Patagonia in South America, crossing the United States on a path that runs along the entire Mississippi River. Approximately 40 percent of all waterfowl in the United States use this flyway. This is a perfect migratory path for birds, having no mountain ranges to impede flight and with ample habitat, food, and water for their various journeys.

Threats to the River—How Resilient Is She?

The Mississippi River is a heavily impacted ecosystem and has been for a long time. All of its stresses are human induced and include biological, chemical, and physical threats to its integrity. Although its diversity gives it resilience, parts of the river's ecosystems have lost their resilience and are severely impacted.

DEAD ZONE

The Mississippi River drains the entire Corn Belt of the United States. More than 80 percent of the total U.S. corn and soybean production is grown in this fertile area. These crops are typically grown as row crops and require high nutrient additions and pesticide applications to maximize production yields. As a result of the cropping systems, much of the topsoil is eroded and eventually contributes to the suspended-solids load of the river. In addition, much of the added nutrients and pesticides is also leached into the river, either attached to the eroded soil or in the runoff and tile drainage.[3]

Nitrogen and phosphorus are nutrients that are added as chemical fertilizers or manure. Because the cost of amending soil is modest and increases yields, excess fertilizer is often applied. The excess nutrients are carried down to the Gulf of Mexico, and in the coastal region off of the mouth of the Mississippi River they stimulate the growth of algae, which depend on the available nitrogen. When these algal blooms die, they are decomposed by microbes, which depletes the water of oxygen—a condition known as hypoxia. This hypoxic zone cannot support fish or invertebrate life and has frequently been called the "dead zone" in the popular press.

The scale of this phenomenon is difficult to grasp—it is so large that it can be seen from outer space. The hypoxia now covers an area larger than the size of the state of New Jersey. It wasn't present at all prior to the 1950s, when the use of chemical fertilizers accelerated.

A number of national studies have been undertaken to assess the causes and determine the reduction targets to remediate this problem. In 1997, the U.S. Environmental Protection Agency (EPA) established the Mississippi River/Gulf of Mexico Watershed Nutrient Task Force. This task force developed an "Integrated Assessment of Hypoxia in the Northern Gulf of Mexico"[4] followed by its "Action Plan for Reducing, Mitigating and Controlling Hypoxia in the Northern Gulf of Mexico."[5] The action plan called for a reduction of the five-year running average of the areal extent of the Gulf of Mexico hypoxic zone to less than 5,000 square kilometers. The U.S. Environmental Protection Agency Science Advisory Board concluded that a 45 percent reduction in both nitrogen and phosphorus loading to the river is needed to reach this goal.

The upper Mississippi basin, which includes Minnesota, is responsible for approximately 31 percent of the nitrogen arriving in the Gulf, and Minnesota is estimated to contribute about 7 percent of the total. Because federal water quality standards are implemented at the state level, there is no adequate integrated management framework for reducing the amount of nitrogen flowing into the Mississippi and down to the Gulf. Such a framework effort might include land conservation programs and economic incentives, as well as regulations. However, no progress has been made toward implementing such a framework.

Two additional threats combine to greatly threaten the biological diversity and integrity of the Mississippi River. These include the biological threat of invasive species and the physical threat of locks and dams. The Mississippi River is home to the largest number of freshwater species of mussels in the world, boasting forty-one different species, although five of these species are federally endangered and several others are threatened. One of the most devastating threats to the native mussels in recent years is the spread of the invasive zebra mussel. They smother the native mussels by blanketing the bottom of the river. The U.S. Fish and Wildlife Service in cooperation with the departments of natural resources of Minnesota and Wisconsin have an aggressive and successful program to recover and reestablish certain mussel species in the parts of the Mississippi where the zebra mussel is not present.

Mussels have a complicated life cycle that requires their larvae to be carried for a period of time by a host fish. Each mussel species has a unique species of host fish as part of its propagation cycle. So a mussel species can be threatened by the loss of their host fish, even if the adult mussels are healthy. Two species of mussel, the ebony shell and the elephant ear, are considered threatened by the federal government because of locks and dams—their specific host fish are physically restricted from migrating to the area where the mussels once reproduced. A concerted effort to reunite the host fish and the mussels, or lock and dam removal, is needed to preserve these two species. Although this need is recognized, no such efforts have proceeded.

WATER CONTAMINANTS

The Mississippi River is impacted by the discharge and runoff of a long list of chemical contaminants in addition to agricultural fertilizers. Much of what is discharged upstream accumulates downstream, so the water quality in New Orleans is significantly deteriorated compared to the water quality in Minneapolis and St Paul.

The contaminants of concern can be placed in three overall categories. The first includes agricultural fertilizers and pesticides; the second includes what are known as "legacy contaminants," which are now regulated or banned but are highly persistent and still cause environmental harm; and the third includes chemicals of emerging concern, which are those contaminants that are not yet well regulated and that recent science has indicated are present in the environment and may cause harm—these include consumer chemicals and plastics additives that can mimic hormones, and human and veterinary pharmaceuticals.

The legacy contaminants of concern are mostly those that bioaccumulate in fish and can cause harm to humans and wildlife after exposure to the contaminants by eating the fish. The chemicals that occur most frequently in fish at harmful levels are polychlorinated biphenyls (PCBS) and methylmercury. PCBS were used in industrial applications from the 1930s into the 1970s but are still found in the environment today and at great enough levels in fish to trigger fish consumption advisories from state health departments up and down the river. Mercury is emitted into the air from coal-fired power plants, enters surface water from rain and runoff, and can be methylated by certain sediment bacteria into the most toxic form of mercury, methylmercury. Methylmercury bioaccumulates readily in fish, and there are state and national fish consumption advisories to prevent too much exposure to mercury. For example, the general public in Minnesota is advised to restrict their consumption of Mississippi River fish to no more than one meal per week. For more susceptible populations, such as children and women of child-bearing age, the advice is to eat no more than one meal of Mississippi River fish per month. These advisories are protective against exposure to both mercury and PCBS.

The contaminants of emerging concern are more numerous and varied in their sources than the legacy contaminants. Many are found in consumer products rather than in industrial discharges, and they find their way into wastewater plants where they are collected and discharged to the environment with little removal or treatment. Examples include the antimicrobial additives that are added to household cleansers; plasticizers that are added to plastic bottles, containers, and canned-food sealants; laundry soap additives used to enhance detergent performance; over-the-counter and prescription medications; and even caffeine from coffee consumption. In addition to wastewater effluents, veterinary pharmaceuticals and hormone enhancement drugs from livestock operations are another source of unwanted contaminants to surface waters, including the agriculturally rich Mississippi River basin. My colleagues and I have studied the occurrence and impacts of hormone-mimicking contaminants in the Mississippi River at St. Paul, and while some of the contaminants are reduced by the wastewater treatment plant process, the discharge is still contaminated enough to cause endocrine disruption in the fish immediately downstream of the treatment plant. Not only do we need to implement treatment technologies to remove these contaminants before they reach the river, we need to "move upstream" in the manufacturer-consumer continuum and prevent the introduction of these contaminants in the first place through green chemistry and consumer education.

Our Heritage, Our Responsibility

The Mississippi River is a complex ecological system, and overlaid on that is an even more complex set of human uses and values. We use the river for drinking water, recreation, commercial fishing, energy, transportation, cooling water, washing wastewater, industrial discharges, and agricultural runoff downstream. It is critical to develop a comprehensive stewardship plan for the river that accounts for its multiple and competing uses in their entirety and respects the many values held by its diverse population. Central to such a plan is to define and implement strategies that optimize these values and uses while minimizing the adverse impacts on the river. The EPA Mississippi River/Gulf of Mexico Watershed Nutrient Task Force action plan and the U.S. EPA Science Advisory Board report contain some of these elements. Ultimately, such an effort will require an interdisciplinary, multistakeholder approach that gets incorporated into a legal framework as well as into our social fabric.

The tragedy of the I-35W bridge collapse and its rapid replacement with a new bridge can serve as a metaphor and lesson for our management of the river. Resilience, restoration, protection, and stewardship are all values that apply to our community and society in general as well as specifically to the river and to the rebuilding of the bridge. The Mississippi River claims Minnesota as its birthplace, and in return we owe the river our commitment to the highest level of stewardship for its present and its future.

NOTES

1.   For a visual representation of the Mississippi River drainage basin, see "Hypoxia in the Northern Gulf of Mexico," Science Advisory Board Report of the U.S. Environmental Protection Agency, EPA-SAB-08-003, http://www.epa.gov/sab.

2.   See http://www.birdnature.com/mississippi.html.

3.   For a satellite image of the Louisiana coast and northern Gulf of Mexico captured by Oceansat-1 using Ocean Color Monitor, see Earth Scan Laboratory, Louisiana State University, http://www.esl.lsu.edu.

4.   See http://oceanservice.noaa.gov/products/pubs_hypox.html.

5.   See http://www.epa.gov/msbasin/taskforce/actionplan.htm.

Reimagining the Mississippi

Patrick Nunnally

When the I-35W bridge collapsed into the Mississippi River in 2007, I was at a birthday party for a friend's daughter. Word spread quickly. There were lots of questions: "Did you hear about the bridge?" "What happened?" "Do you think it was terrorists?" People asked me one question in particular, perhaps because they know I work on river-related issues: Where is it?

For the life of me, I couldn't place the bridge and where it crossed the river. It had not yet become a "place" in my imagination of the urban Twin Cities Mississippi River corridor. Now, of course, that crossing is prominent in my mental map of the river in Minneapolis.

The gap in my geographical imagination was partly because I rarely used the bridge. My routes in and around the city almost never took me on I-35W. On the few occasions when I was on that route, I was generally either north or south of the river crossing. Like city dwellers everywhere, I had my set routes and little routines for getting around my home turf. In my daily encounters with the river, I mostly travel—by car, bicycle, and walking—along the river rather than across it.

My failure to place the collapsed bridge is also partly because of the way it was designed. The highway bridge didn't feel like a bridge, as I have heard over and over from people who did drive it. The few times I crossed the old bridge, I could never tell precisely when my car left the highway proper and was actually on the bridge structure. I remember years ago, when my son was small, he and his buddies played a game where they held their breath during the entire duration of a trip across any bridge. The old I-35W bridge frustrated them because they could never tell when to start and stop their game.

More substantively, though, I think my failure to place the I-35W crossing of the Mississippi River is part of a broader failure in the Twin Cities: we haven't really come to terms with the Mississippi as part of our urban fabric. Oh sure, we cross it, and more recently we have begun to take some pride in it. But I don't think we have fully reimagined it, brought it into our mental constructs of who we are and where we live. Minneapolis is the "City of Lakes" and Minnesota is the "Land of 10,000 Lakes." But if you go nearly anywhere in the world and try to explain where Minnesota is, you get the first moment of recognition when you say that Minnesota is where the Mississippi River begins.

What might it mean to reimagine the river, how might that happen, and what would it mean for us, for our cities, and for the river itself? Before we explore those questions, let's look back through the past thirty or so years of riverfront revitalization work that, important though it is, I believe sets the stage for the broader reimagining that is necessary for us to develop a three-hundred-year relationship with the Mississippi.

Why three hundred years? New Orleans was established in 1718, so 2018 therefore marks the tricentennial of westernized urban development along the Mississippi River. I think this is also an important time line for consideration of our future on this river: What will our river cities be like in 2318? Will they be any more sustainable than they are today? We've started down the path toward a vision of an urban river that will be healthy and part of a healthy city, and, I shall argue, there is important work taking place now that will take us further on that path. But we aren't there yet.

The Mississippi as the Front Door of Minneapolis and St. Paul

Like most river cities in the United States, Minneapolis and St. Paul grew up because of the geographical particulars of their locations: Minneapolis was at the Mississippi's largest waterpower source, St. Anthony Falls, and St. Paul was the head of steamboat navigation on the Mississippi. The river was their front door, but it was also dirty, polluted, and dangerous, not an elegant, welcoming place. With the advent of railroads and alternatives to hydropower, the cities gradually turned their backs on the river, although still utilizing it for removal of waste and, albeit decreasingly, for transportation. During the first three-quarters of the twentieth century, the Mississippi was a no-man's-land, a gash cut through the heart of the cities.

This situation began to change with the passage of the Clean Water Act and the removal of the last industrial-scale milling from the Minneapolis riverfront. Following the 1972 release of their first riverfront plan, *Mississippi/Minneapolis*, Minneapolis city officials dedicated staff and development incentives to restoring the riverfront. In the early years, efforts concentrated on removing barriers to development such as pollution, obsolete industrial and transportation-related land uses, and simply promoting the riverfront as an important part of the city. For many, the keystone project that marked a pivotal point in decades of effort was the rehabilitation of the Stone Arch Bridge from an abandoned railway bridge to a pedestrian-bicycling facility. This link in what was rapidly becoming a network of trail opportunities allowed people to see both banks of the river as connected by an easy bike ride, stroll, or jog. The Stone Arch Bridge reopened in 1994 and kicked off a decade of renewed public investment in projects such as Mill Ruins Park and the completion of parkways, bikeways, and park land throughout the area. The historic landmark Washburn Crosby mill, damaged by fire in 1991, opened as the $24 million Mill City Museum in 2003, managed by the Minnesota Historical Society. The renowned Guthrie Theater relocated to the riverfront, opening in 2006. Meanwhile hundreds of housing units opened, mostly concentrated at the higher end of the price spectrum, and the central riverfront became truly a diverse, vibrant part of the city. By 2007, thirty-five years after the first planning/vision document was published, public investment of nearly $400 million had leveraged an estimated $1.4 billion in private capital.[1]

Downriver, St. Paul started its riverfront renaissance later and organized its work slightly differently. St. Paul is governed by a strong mayor system of government, with the executive having dominion over departments such as public works, planning, and parks. As opposed to Minneapolis, with a strong city council and an independent park board, St. Paul can respond much more quickly and decisively to events. When a substantial private employer in St. Paul decamped to the suburbs in the early 1990s, the city leaders questioned how the city would thrive in the future as employment began to leave the city. Their answer was to focus on St. Paul's relationship to the Mississippi River. Publication in 1997 of the *St. Paul on the Mississippi Development Framework*[2] stimulated important public investment, such as the $14 million rehabilitation of Harriet Island Regional Park and private projects such as the $140 million Upper Landing residential and mixed-use development. In St. Paul, the widely regarded catalytic event was undertaken privately: the decision in the late 1990s by the Science Museum of Minnesota to relocate to the riverfront and build a $100 million destination attraction there. Like Minneapolis, recreation has been an important component of the overall work; when completed in 2004, the Sam Morgan Regional Trail became a key link in a system of nearly one hundred miles of riverfront bikeways in the region.

Over these past years of activity, two clear visions of the urban riverfront have emerged. Some see the Mississippi River as the great, green heart of the city, the trunk corridor that connects creeks and streams, patterns of recreational trails, and other components of what some call "green infrastructure." This concept may be thought of as an update of the vision articulated over a century ago by the landscape architect Horace William Shaler Cleveland, who laid out the Minneapolis system of Grand Rounds, parkways encircling some of the city's major lakes and connected by a parkway network.

Others see the Mississippi River as the most prominent urban design, planning, economic development, and political corridor in the region. They point to the establishment of attractions like the Guthrie Theater and the fact that the highest-valued houses in St. Paul are no longer on Summit Avenue but along River Boulevard. Proponents of this vision point out that the Twin Cities were established because of the Mississippi and that their presence in the post-whatever-this-economy-is will be due to how well they take advantage of their place along the river.

Reimagining the Mississippi

These are both powerful visions, and although they are often posed as an either/or opposition, I would argue that ultimately they both need to be pushed forward. The river's natural systems, and the investments that have made them accessible to the public through systems of trails and open space, are important components of why property values along the river are among the highest in the region. And the development that takes place along the corridor puts tax money into public coffers, thereby allowing the investment in public amenities to continue. From 1972 through 2007, the cycle was generally spiraling up, albeit with some downturns. The economic downturn that began in 2007 and reached such dramatic and public forms in 2008 is a lesson to old hands on the river that this is a time to plan for when the economy turns back up. In the coming period of growth, whenever the recession ends, we can either continue as we have gone, planning incrementally, taking whatever development projects look best at the time, and hoping that it will all work out in the long term, or we can do otherwise, planning with long-term vision—the three-hundred-year sustainability vision—always in mind. That's our reimagination of the river. Our imagination of the river in its urban setting must encompass three understandings.

First, we should see the river as water. The Mississippi River is, above all, a river, a body of moving water that functions more or less well according to hydrological patterns, that serves more or less well as a source of drinking and other water needs for the human population along its banks, and that serves, again, more or less well as habitat for fish and other important ecological species. In the language of some scientists, the river provides important "ecosystem services," but it is also an important and threatened body of water, regardless of the services it provides to humans.

Second, we should see the river as urban design. The Mississippi is central to how the Twin Cities of Minneapolis and St. Paul have grown over the past several decades. As that planning and design continue to progress, as we design as if the river mattered, we'll understand more clearly and more thoroughly that the Mississippi River once again is the front door to the region after being our back door and mudroom for so long.

Finally, we should imagine the river as home. The Mississippi River has for millennia been inseparable from the lives of many people along its banks. Indigenous people lived here; and after Europeans and Americans came, it was the place where many people made their homes. Those stories are little known and perhaps may play an important role in our future efforts to redefine ourselves in relation to the river.

THE RIVER AS WATER

For most people in the Twin Cities, water comes from a tap. When we want water, we turn a handle or a valve, and there it is. When we're done with it, whether used for cleaning, for bathing, for sanitary purposes, or what have you, it simply goes down the drain and disappears.

We do think about water occasionally. On hot days in summer, some of us like to go out in a boat on the Mississippi or on a lake. In drought conditions, such as we have had sporadically over the past few years, there may be a news story about the water level in the river dropping near the intake plant for the Minneapolis water treatment facility. But we never think about what might happen if it dropped enough to affect our supply.

Likewise with pollution. We know vaguely that the river is polluted, not fishable and swimmable as the goals of the Clean Water Act require. And again, there is the occasional news story about water pollution being traced to a particular factory or the establishment of trace chemical residues that are finding their way into fish with harmful consequences. Activists among us may spend an afternoon stenciling "Don't Pollute" warnings on storm drains in our neighborhoods. Experts understand that the river is "impaired," to use the language of the Clean Water Act, with regard to nutrients, sediment, and bacteria, but as long as the city's drinking water filters work properly, this is, at best, abstract knowledge.

We have no real sense of how we depend on the Mississippi or how we may or may not be in peril from trace pollution or other issues. We have very little sense that millions of people downstream from us depend on the river for their water needs.

In the Twin Cities recently, there have been concerns about the use of the river for power and transportation. To some extent, these arguments echo uses of the river for the past 150 years, but in important ways they reflect the need to imagine the river for the twenty-first century.

Although the heyday of river transportation peaked in about the 1870s, St. Paul remains an important commercial shipping point, at least from there and to and from points downstream. The St. Anthony Falls locks and dams, though, have seen decreasing use over the past decade. Strident voices call for the removal of the two locks and dams at the falls and for the removal of the lock and hydroelectric plant near the Ford truck factory a few miles farther downriver. But can the dams simply be removed? What lies behind them in terms of sediments along the river bottom, and what would happen to those sediments if they were released downriver? Would removal of the dams really result in greater fish passage for sturgeon and walleye? What about the dreaded Asian carp? Also, if there were eventually no more barge traffic upstream from the confluence with the Minnesota, would the removal of dams allow for a better recreation experience for canoeists and kayakers? Would the rapids that are described so often by nineteenth-century explorers return?

The answers to these questions are not simple, despite the ardent hopes of some advocates. The McKnight Foundation, whose environment program has poured millions of dollars into Mississippi River restoration since the mid-1990s, recently awarded a grant to the University of Minnesota to conduct background research into the management frameworks that govern the river in the Mississippi gorge area as well as scientific precedents and studies concerning hydrology, river ecology, and other factors that are affected by water-level management. Specifically, have other strategies, such as temporary drawdowns, channel creation, and island building, been used in other rivers or other sections of the Mississippi in order to restore ecological function, and what have the effects been? Preliminary results indicate there are no areas quite like the urban Mississippi where such efforts have been made; most have taken place on smaller, more rural streams. But it does appear that potentially there are ways to restore certain ecological functions without resorting, initially at least, to dam removal.

The McKnight-sponsored gorge study will give us a much more nuanced appreciation for what is possible in our relation to the river. Instead of the either/or thinking that says we can have an ecologically functioning river or a river that meets human needs, greater knowledge of the river's hydrology, chemistry, ecology, and our impacts on those qualities will allow the Mississippi to become a multifunctional river. A greater understanding of subtle impacts will allow us to use the river without diminishing it. Studies such as this one will allow us to know a lot more about the way the river works as a river, in addition to how we make it a working river, serving our needs not just as ecosystem services but also for the improved quality of human life.

THE RIVER AS URBAN DESIGN

There are a number of projects in both Minneapolis and St. Paul that have pointed the city back toward the river. The St. Anthony Falls Heritage Board, created by state law in 1988 to safeguard the historic resources at the Minneapolis Central Riverfront and to find the right balance between heritage preservation and the needs of a vibrant city, has recently undertaken a comprehensive look at how the area is interpreted to the public. It has become apparent to the consultants conducting the study and to the staff task force working with them that interpretation is far more complex than just deciding what should be written on a set of markers. The team is asking: Who is the audience for interpretation and who comes to the Heritage District? Who do we want to address? If certain groups, such as recent immigrants, families with children, and young adults, do not frequent the historic district, are there remedies that would make the district more welcoming to all segments of the population? A critically important realization has been that interpretation is not just a matter of signs or engaging storytelling. Telling river stories, particularly if we want to engage youth and their families who do not traditionally come to the area for recreation, means removing obstacles to their feeling welcome. Interpretation, as tied to place making, becomes integral to urban design.

Among the most vexing questions facing planners is the issue of how to build on the area's outstanding physical assets: massive nineteenth-century stone flour mills, intimate pockets of still natural landscapes, and the river itself. Instead of regarding ecological restoration as competing with historic preservation, how can the two perspectives be integrated to their mutual benefit? How can the deeply understood sense of place held by many indigenous people be conveyed in a manner that is respectful and allows native voices to be fully heard? Finally, how can these three perspectives—indigenous knowledge, ecological function, and historic resource preservation— all be integrated into a growing city?

So far, a clear precedent or model for this complex charge has not emerged. Certainly places like Boston have some of the desired attributes, but planners have not yet found one that contains all three—indigenous sensibilities, attention to ecological processes, and historic built form—in a vital city. The expected benefit is to develop a plan and blueprint to guide public investment for the next twenty years. It is hard to think about a three-hundred-year horizon with political timetables and the vagaries of the market, but the agencies that make up the Heritage Board have done it before. However, their work is not yet finished.

Understanding the river as home may not be so much about getting people to see the fact of the river as it is about broadening the
reach of the people who do see it. Preliminary audience research conducted on behalf of the St. Anthony Falls Heritage Board shows that
many local communities of color don't think of the river much at all.
Indigenous people who are still here after decades of what can be
described as warfare against their culture may not feel welcome and
may not feel that their understandings of the river, which are complex and stretch back millennia, will be respected. Understanding the
river as home is not a panacea, of course. But it can offer what the
historian Dolores Hayden in her book *The Power of Place* calls a recognition of our common humanity that can

> acknowledge and respect diversity, while reaching beyond
> multiple and sometimes conflicting national, ethnic, gen-
> der, race, and class identities to encompass larger common
> themes, such as the migration experience, the breakdown
> and reformulation of families, or the search for a new sense
> of identity in an urban setting.[3]

One way to approach Hayden's vision is to use art to build concern
for the river among the whole population rather than the usual
audience of white, middle-class people who already have a disposition toward river recreation or "green" sensibilities. Young people
from disadvantaged communities within the Twin Cities have been
involved in restoration of Mississippi River natural areas for years
through programs of the Community Design Center of Minnesota.
The long-standing East Side Conservation Corps program in St. Paul
brings together youth from the city's Hmong, Hispanic, and African
American communities with gardeners and nonprofit restoration
ecologists to clear invasive vegetation species and replant areas of
the Bruce Vento Nature Sanctuary. In 2008, the concept expanded to
Minneapolis, where a Green Team[4] of youth worked with staff from
the National Park Service Mississippi National River and Recreation
Area, the Minneapolis Park and Recreation Board, and the Mississippi

FIGURE 9.1 » Ceramics artist Anna Metcalfe *(back row, far right)* and students on the Minneapolis Green Team with their "story boats" at Father Hennepin Bluffs Park, Minneapolis. Photograph courtesy of Anna Metcalfe.

FIGURE 9.2 » "Story boats," artistic collaborations between ceramics artist Anna Metcalfe and students on the Minneapolis Green Team, summer 2008. Photograph courtesy of Anna Metcalfe.

Watershed Management Organization to begin ecological restoration work at the Father Hennepin Bluffs Park, located on the east side of St. Anthony Falls.

Ceramic artist Anna Metcalfe, a graduate student earning her MFA at the University of Minnesota, approached project coordinators in early summer with a new idea: why not ask the program's members to draw and write their "river story" on paper outlines of boat shapes, which Metcalfe would then fire into a series of "story boats," each illustrating an individual's expressive relationship to the Mississippi River? The coordinators agreed that the expressive opportunity offered by the story boat project provided the students a chance to reflect in a different way about their evolving relationship with the river that they had been working with all summer. Metcalfe held workshops for both the Minneapolis and St. Paul teams, collected their drawings and writings, and fired a series of clay boats, nearly sixty in all.

Toward the end of the summer, students had the opportunity to see their boats as artistic objects, co-created between themselves and Metcalfe. Many of the drawings were exquisite, and the stories contained quite moving accounts of the students' ongoing emotional and personal attachment to the river.

What do we achieve if more of us understand the river as home? For one thing, broadening the range of people who care for the river is essential to our having a long-term healthy relationship with it. Building engagement with the river is vital to our future life with it, and that engagement must go beyond traditional stakeholders. The river runs through all of us, and all of us should care for it.

Now What?

If all of this work is going on, and the cities have taken such important steps toward a twenty-first-century riverfront, what's next? I believe three considerations should remain prominent for planners, agencies, and policy makers.

We need more research. We don't yet know as much as we need to about how a large, complex urban river such as the Mississippi actually works. The research must go beyond the conventional nature/city divide that sees human places as inevitably corrupt and focuses only on the ecological processes of wild areas. We must learn, and soon, what benefits the river provides us, both those we are already aware of, such as clean water, and those that may not be known yet. As the population of the region grows and our climate changes, how will our metropolitan health be dependent on a healthy river? What *is* a healthy river in a metropolitan area?

We need to get and keep the attention of people not currently engaged in the river's future. The river must be understood to run through all of us, not just those who have leisure to play on it or who identify with its history. The necessary continued investment in the river's future will only come when there is broad-based public demand that the river remain central to our sense of ourselves.

All of our projects need evaluation and assessment to ensure that we are meeting the goals we set. It's a great start to hear people talk about the triple bottom line (environmental and social benefits as well as economic values), but we must have more precise ways to understand the value of the public and private investment on the urban riverfront. The Sustainable Sites Initiative[5] offers one set of emerging models, but greater concentration on a sustainable economy is needed as well. The Sustainable Sites Initiative is an interdisciplinary effort by the American Society of Landscape Architects, the Lady Bird Johnson Wildflower Center, and the U.S. Botanic Garden to create voluntary national guidelines and performance benchmarks for sustainable land design, construction and maintenance practices. Think of LEED[6] beyond buildings. The benchmarks developed by this effort are necessary tools, but until a sustainable economic model for urban growth emerges, and the political will coalesces to undertake a pattern of development as if the river matters, benchmarks are just stopgaps, not transformative.

The collapse of the I-35W bridge brought the Mississippi River to the forefront of the Twin Cities' imagination of themselves, albeit in a tragic way and just for a few months. A new bridge was built in record time because all of the agencies, political jurisdictions, and, indeed, the public, demanded concerted action. A similar concerted set of actions, only carried out over a longer period of time and involving a great many more participants, will be necessary to develop a twenty-first-century urban riverfront. The effort, cost, and dedication required will be great, but the reward is potentially great as well. Minneapolis and St. Paul, two great cities on a great river, can become known as the first cities in the world to be places where their river carries fish and people, where the connections of human and ecological systems are deeply healing of people, land, community, and the river that connects us all.

NOTES

1.   *Minneapolis Riverfront Revitalization: Three Decades of Progress*, http://www.ci.minneapolis.mn.us/cped/docs/Riverfront_PowerPoint.pdf (2007, with updates through 2009).

2.   *St. Paul on the Mississippi Development Framework* (1997), http://www.riverfrontcorporation.com/?page_id=529.

3.   Dolores Hayden, *The Power of Place: Urban Landscapes as Public History* (Cambridge, Mass.: MIT Press, 1995), 9.

4.   The Green Team is a group of disadvantaged Minneapolis youth who have been brought together in the summer to conduct habitat restoration work along the Mississippi.

5.   The Sustainable Sites Initiative, http://www.sustainablesites.org/.

6.   Leadership in Energy and Environmental Design (LEED) is a program of the U.S. Green Building Council that is widely accepted as a measure of sustainability in buildings.

ACKNOWLEDGMENTS

This project came together through the timely and ongoing efforts of many people. Deb Swackhamer, Judith Martin, and Ann Waltner were involved in the group that first formulated the notion of a course and lecture series on the bridge collapse and aftermath. Jon Binks in the Provost's Office was helpful in making the course and lectures possible. Planning for the fall 2008 symposium included all of these individuals plus representatives from the University of Minnesota Press. Contributions to that symposium came from Jon Foley and Patricia Hampl, in addition to the authors of the essays included here. Many thanks are due the authors for their revision and dedication to seeing the project come to fruition.

The untimely death of our friend and colleague Roger Miller while this book was in press has saddened us. It is a personal reminder of what was at stake for so many in the bridge collapse.

John O. Anfinson is a historian with the Mississippi National River and Recreation Area, a unit of the National Park Service. He is a founding board member of Friends of the Mississippi River, an organization that focuses on the environmental health of the Mississippi in the Twin Cities area. He is the author of *The River We Have Wrought: A History of the Upper Mississippi* (Minnesota, 2003) and *River of History: A Historic Resources Study of the Mississippi National River and Recreation Area.*

Roberto Ballarini is James L. Record Professor and head of the Department of Civil Engineering at the University of Minnesota. His research focuses on the mechanics of fracture and fatigue of materials and structures.

Heather Dorsey teaches speech communication and theater arts classes for freshmen and sophomores in the College of Education at the University of Minnesota. Her areas of instruction include live performance and stage direction. She also works as a performer and director at theaters around the Twin Cities.

Thomas Fisher is professor and dean of the College of Design at the University of Minnesota. He previously served as the editorial director of *Progressive Architecture* magazine and has lectured or juried at many schools and professional societies. He is the author of several books, including *In the Scheme of Things: Alternative Thinking on the Practice of Architecture* (Minnesota, 2000); *Salmela Architect* (Minnesota, 2005); *The Invisible Element of Place* (Minnesota, 2011); and *Architectural Design and Ethics: Tools for Survival.*

Minmao Liao is a doctoral candidate in the Department of Civil Engineering at the University of Minnesota. He received his BS and MS in civil engineering from Tsinghua University in Beijing, China.

Judith A. Martin is professor of geography, director of the urban studies program, and former codirector of the University Metropolitan Consortium at the University of Minnesota. Her major publications analyze urban planning efforts, neighborhood development, historic preservation, and urban renewal. Her recent writing focuses on metropolitan governance, city planning, and urban design.

Roger Miller was associate professor of geography at the University of Minnesota. His interests were in the history of planning, comparative international planning with an emphasis on Scandinavia, and urbanization.

Patrick Nunnally is coordinator of the River Life program, part of the University of Minnesota's Institute on the Environment. He works with diverse groups to integrate resource protection and place-based interpretation into ongoing local and regional planning frameworks. He teaches landscape planning and urban studies at the University of Minnesota.

Mark Pedelty is associate professor in the School of Journalism and Mass Communication at the University of Minnesota. His ethnographic media research has been conducted in Central America, Mexico, and Minnesota. He is the author of two books and numerous articles concerning media, politics, and performance.

E. Thomas Sullivan is senior vice president for Academic Affairs and Provost and the Julius E. Davis Chair in Law at the University of Minnesota.

Deborah L. Swackhamer is professor and Charles M. Denny Jr. Chair in Science, Technology, and Public Policy in the Hubert H. Humphrey Institute of Public Affairs, and codirector of the Water Resources Center at the University of Minnesota. She currently serves as chair of the Science Advisory Board for the U.S. Environmental Protection Agency and is an appointed member of the Minnesota Clean Water Council.

Melissa Thompson is a doctoral candidate in the School of Journalism and Mass Communication at the University of Minnesota. Her research focuses on environmental and food production issues.